PURITY OF DICTION IN
ENGLISH VERSE

PURITY OF DICTION
IN ENGLISH VERSE

Donald Davie

SCHOCKEN BOOKS · NEW YORK

To Doreen

Acknowledgments

Some parts of this book have previously appeared in *The Cambridge Journal*, *Hermathena* and *Essays in Criticism*. My thanks are due to the editors of these journals for permission to reproduce material which first figured in their pages.

Acknowledgment is also made to the Oxford University Press for permission to print the extracts from *The Letters of Gerard Manley Hopkins to Robert Bridges*, *The Correspondence of Gerard Manley Hopkins and Richard Watson Dixon*, and *Further Letters of Gerard Manley Hopkins* quoted in Part II, Chapter IV.

D. A. D.

CONTENTS

CONTENTS

INTRODUCTION

Some time ago I began to read the works of some English poets who lived in the middle and towards the close of the eighteenth century. I was surprised and pleased to find how much I enjoyed them; but I found it hard to rationalize the enjoyment they gave me. With most of my contemporaries, I thought that the surest sign of poetic greatness was the ability to organize experience by apt and memorable metaphor. Suitably qualified, this is still my belief. But to make those qualifications, and to account for the respect I felt, I have had to go a long way round. My difficulties hinged on the question: whether it is true that in the eighteenth century literary English was metaphorically impoverished. In the last hundred years most literary historians have found this metaphorical poverty falling, like a shadow, over most English poetry written between the death of Pope and the publication of *Lyrical Ballads*. I have come to believe that what seems poverty is sometimes economy; and that this economy in metaphor produces effects which I call 'poetical', to which, it seems to me, most readers of our day are blind. The effects seem to me to be morally valuable; otherwise I should not care to write of them.

I have spent much time trying to understand what is meant by the 'diction' of poetry. But I am interested in the problem of diction only so as to use that notion, where no other will meet the case, in appreciating certain poetry of the past and the present. I derive from this poetry a pleasure which I can only describe by saying that the diction is pure. I feel, when I read some other poetry, a peculiar discomfort which I can define only by saying that the diction is impure. I want to understand what I mean when I make these judgments. I want to know how the poet goes about to produce this kind of pleasure, and what is its moral value for the reader. I do not offer the notion of purity in diction as an ultimate criterion of the worth of poetry. I know some valuable poems, especially of the nineteenth century, which suffer, as I think, from an impure diction; and I regret the discomfort which this causes, while admitting a counter-balance of virtues (that is, useful pleasures) of another order or another kind. Again, I find many great poems to which the notions of purity or impurity in diction seem merely irrelevant. I do not argue for a new criterion, only for an old one which has fallen out of use. This criterion is not equally relevant to all sorts of English poetry or in all phases of the English poetic tradition. I am interested in it because I think it relevant, indeed indispensable, to the poetry of Goldsmith's contemporaries, and to that of my own.

Of the essays which follow, those in Part I are devoted to defining and exemplifying the principles of purity in diction, with reference for the most part to poetry of the later eighteenth century; in the remainder I attempt to apply these principles to some later poetry, or to show how later criticism could find no room for them. The essays in Part II are self-contained, more provocative and probably more questionable in their conclusions than those in Part I, where I try to follow a consecutive argument through several chapters.

PART I

I

THE DICTION OF ENGLISH VERSE

A FRIEND asks me what I stand to gain from talking about 'the diction of verse', instead of 'the language of poetry'. For him, these are two ways of saying one thing, and my way is only the more pretentious. Now it seems to me that it would be pretentious to talk about the 'diction' of Gerard Manley Hopkins, and faintly precious, even, to talk of his 'verse'. If 'diction' is a selection from the language of men, then Hopkins may be said to use a poetic diction in the ridiculous sense that 'hogshead' or any other word one may call to mind was never used by him in any of his poems, and that he therefore used a selection of the language which excluded 'hogshead' or whatever word it is. But the point is that in reading the poems of Hopkins one has no sense of English words thrusting to be let into the poem and held out of it by the poet. One feels that Hopkins could have found a place for every word in the language if only he could have written enough poems. One feels the same about Shakespeare. But there are poets, I find, with whom I feel the other thing—that a selection has been made and is continually being made, that words are thrusting at the poem and being fended off from it, that however many poems these poets wrote certain words would never be allowed into the poems, except as a disastrous oversight. These different feelings we have, when we read English poetry, justify us in talking of the language of the one kind of poet, and the diction of the other kind, of the poetry of the one and the verse of the other.

We cannot help feeling that verse is somehow less important and splendid than poetry, just as diction is less splendid than language. And I think this is right. To begin with, nearly all bad poets (we have to except the lunatic fringe) use a poetic diction. And usually we cannot deny that what they write is verse, although we would strenuously deny that it is poetry. Everyone knows why bad poets use a poetic diction. The worst poets of all have no sense for words; but most poets are sufficiently sensitive to recognize the words which are fashionable. There are fashions in words for poetry, as in words for conversation, and out of the words that are fashionable every age constructs willy-nilly its own poetic diction, which the bad poets (unconsciously for the most part) adopt. An example of such a fashionable word in our own time is 'improbable'—'the trees' improbable green', 'Islands improbably remote'. It is relatively easy to recognize bad poetic diction. It is more difficult to understand that poetic diction can be good, to recognize good diction, and to distinguish it from the bad.

Presumably, if a bad diction is the result of selecting from the language at random, according to the whim of fashion, then good diction comes from making a selection from the language on reasonable principles and for a reasonable purpose. All poets when they write have one purpose. They want to create an effect upon the mind of the reader. These effects are various, and the poets dispute about which effects are legitimate and worth-while. When the poets and critics are very sure about what effects are legitimate, then they can construct a very elaborate structure of poetic diction, as it were departmentalized, according to the different effects which the poet may legitimately seek to produce. Such an elaborate structure was outlined by George Puttenham in the sixteenth century. Puttenham will tell the poet what sort of words, images, measures and rhymes he must adopt in order to produce any one of the effects which Puttenham considers legitimate. Since Puttenham's day this elaborate structure has been broken down more and more, as the poets in practice have blurred the distinctions upon which that structure rested. By the time that Goldsmith and Wordsworth write of poetic diction, they only occasionally remember that there is more than one sort of poetry. Goldsmith in his essays often pulls himself up short to pay his respects to Ossian, remembering that, besides his own poetry of sentiment, aiming at the effect of pathos, there is a poetry of passion, aiming at the sublime. But Wordsworth only once remembers, in his Appendix to the Preface to the *Lyrical Ballads*, to limit all his remarks to "works *of imagination and sentiment*, for of these only have I been treating". Both Goldsmith sometimes and Wordsworth usually seem to be laying down the law about diction for all sorts of poetry seeking all sorts of effects. Coleridge, when he tried to reply to Wordsworth, in the last chapters of *Biographia Literaria*, attempted to rebuild some of the elaborate structure of Puttenham. He talks about different departments of language and different styles working in these departments. But Coleridge's distinctions and classifications have the air of being made *ad hoc*, and English criticism

7

has preferred in this respect to follow Wordsworth. Nowadays there seems to be nothing to choose between a slack catholicism, which implies that every poem in its kind is as good as every other poem in another kind, and a dogmatic purism, which says, "This good poem is written in this way. Therefore all good poems must be written in this way."

Words like 'lyric', 'satire', 'epic' are remnants of an old elaborate structure in which we no longer believe. And as forty years ago it often seemed that all poems had to be lyrics, so now it often seems that they must all be satires. It is not to be expected that the old elaborate classifications will be restored in their old strength and minuteness. And perhaps it is just as well. For it may be doubted whether a modern poet could write with the conscious art of Spenser. And even in Spenser's day the schemes of diction seem to have produced pedantic and self-opinionated readers. On the other hand it may be doubted whether criticism can improve unless it can breathe life into some of the old classifications.

Related to this distinction by genres is distinction by tone. Goldsmith provides an example:

Homer has been blamed for the bad choice of his similes on some particular occasions. He compares Ajax to an ass, in the *Iliad*, and Ulysses to a steak broiling on the coals, in the *Odyssey*. His admirers have endeavoured to excuse him, by reminding us of the simplicity of the age in which he wrote; but they have not been able to prove that any ideas of dignity or importance were, even in those days, affixed to the character of an ass, or the quality of a beef collop; therefore they were very improper illustrations for any situation in which a hero ought to be represented.

It is important to realize how we differ from Goldsmith on this count. We cannot deny that there is such a thing as bathos; and I think we must agree that when we compare an eminent man to a broiling steak we run a risk of bathos. We only question whether the prime object of Homer or the epic poet in general, is the dignifying of his heroes; or else perhaps we have different ideas of human dignity. J. M. Synge condemned poetic diction in the Preface to his *Poems and Translations*; poems which were experiments, as it must seem to us, in poetic diction of an unusually elaborate and eccentric kind. In making a diction out of the talk of Irish peasantry, Synge deliberately exploited the bathetic, because he believed "that before verse can be human again it must learn to be brutal". Goldsmith, however, believed that man was human and dignified when he was least brutal, and so it was right for him to complain that human dignity was affronted when compared with the brutish ass. When brutal or vulgar references were inescapable, the eighteenth-century poet preserved a lofty tone by circumlocution. Every poet does the same, when he is working in a lofty vein. Only Wordsworth sometimes refused—often with ludicrous results.

But diction varies in another way. Not only does any given diction vary according to genre (i.e. according to the effect the poet wishes to produce) and according to tone, but one scheme or structure of diction will vary from another, because of the different cultures from which they spring. Synge differs from Goldsmith about diction because he has a different scheme of morality. Thus it is possible to speak of a courtly-humanist diction (Spenser perhaps) and of a bourgeois-pious diction (Samuel Johnson). It seems as if the poet's choice of diction is determined in part, at any rate, by the structure and the prevailing ideologies of his society. If this is so, then the only diction which can be right for a modern poet is the sort of diction which his own society throws out, that is to say, the diction which we have already seen coming out of changes in fashion.

But it can be argued that here the good artist of modern times differs from the masters of the past. André Malraux sees the world of the modern artist as 'le musée imaginaire', upon the walls of which hang examples of all the styles of the past. These styles the modern artist has learnt to appreciate independent of the different cultures of which they were the flowers; and he can choose among them at will, seeking the one he shall use as a model. I think this is largely true, though the artist is still determined by his society to some extent. Yeats must have found in the Irish culture of his time some points of contact with the noble culture of Japan, or the courtly culture of Spenser. Otherwise, I believe, he could not have adopted, even though he modified, the styles of the Japanese theatre and of Spenser's poetry. Still, it must be admitted that the poet to-day has a greater freedom of choice than the poet of the sixteenth century or even of the eighteenth. It is a freedom for which he has to pay dearly, since it is part and parcel of his isolated position in his civilization. But I have to believe that he has this wider measure of freedom, in order to explain the strain of serious parody which runs through so much of the best poetry of our age. For the best modern poems often read as if they were good translations from another language.

But the contemporary poet will not ask what words, arranged in what ways, are suitable for elegy; what other words and arrangements are proper to the ode. He will not ask whether his diction should be courtly and humanist, or heroic and pagan, or bourgeois and pious, or whatever else. He wants to know why he should use a diction at all, why he should exclude from his poetry any of the language with which he is familiar. For him it is axiomatic that "there are no poetical and no unpoetical words". Now, certainly all words are potentially poetical; the achievement of Shakespeare is proof of that. On the other hand it is plain from Goldsmith's essay that for him the language was divided into poetical and unpoetical words. There was a disputed margin in which occurred words and arrangements poetical in some genres, unpoetical in others; but Goldsmith never doubts that some expressions are inherently more poetical than others, and of course it is plain that this conviction governed his practice. It may be agreed that our sense of this principle at work in his verse causes us to rate it below Shakespeare's. But it does not follow that Goldsmith achieved what he did in verse, in spite of an erroneous opinion. It may have been the condition of his doing what it did. Perhaps it was not erroneous, for him. There may be some poets for whom "there are no poetical and no unpoetical words"; it may be equally true that for other poets, some words are poetical while others are not.

It may even be true (I think it is) that the poet who works in Goldsmith's way can compass certain effects, or at least one effect, which is not possible even for a Shakespeare. Shakespeare does many things that Goldsmith cannot do; but Goldsmith does at least one thing that Shakespeare cannot do. This one effect, which can be compassed by verse and not by poetry, has already been described—as a sense of "words thrusting to be let into the poem, but fended off from it". It remains to be seen at a later stage what moral value can be derived from this effect, by the reader who enjoys it.

The poet who creates a style should not, perhaps, be said to write *in* that style. At any rate, there is no Miltonic diction in Milton; there is only Milton's style. For Miltonic diction we go to Thomson. There is no Chaucerian diction in Chaucer; for that we go to some poems by Dunbar. Anyone who thinks otherwise is that famous reader who found Gray's Elegy 'full of quotations'. Not Chaucer nor Milton nor Pope can be said to employ a diction. They create styles, which is a different matter; and it is a sort of historical accident that later poets should have drawn upon their styles to make up a poetic diction.

Even so, there is a difference between imitating a style and observing a diction. For only bad poets, I think, use a diction taken over, lock, stock and barrel, from the style of a previous poet. At this point the discussion has been bedevilled by Wordsworth. For every schoolboy knows that Wordsworth disliked poetic diction and decided, instead, to write in a selection of the language really used by men. But nearly every schoolboy knows, too, that this is what diction is—a selection from the language commonly used. And it is a fact that when we read the criticism of such poets as Johnson and

Goldsmith (who use a diction which we think we can recognize), we find that they appeal, not to literary precedent alone, but to spoken usage:

> Gray thought his language more poetical as it was more re-
> mote from common use: finding in Dryden *honey redolent of*
> *Spring*, an expression that reaches the utmost limits of our
> language, Gray drove it a little more beyond apprehension by
> making *gales* to be *redolent of joy and youth*.

Here there is certainly appeal to the practice of a past master; but there is, at least equally, an appeal to 'common use'.

It may be questioned, perhaps, whether this 'common use', to which Johnson appeals, is indeed spoken usage and not, rather, the usage of prose-writing. And it is certainly important to ask whether he appeals equally to the spoken usage of Gin Lane, of Grub Street, of the Cumbrian fells and of Mrs. Thrale's drawing-room. But to any sympathetic reader of Johnson's verse, and the verse of his age, such questions turn out to be (except for some rather peculiar cases[1]) only quibbles. Everyone must agree with Coleridge that poetic language, however conversational in origin, must be arranged with a care unusual in any but the most studied speaking;[2] and hence the distinction,

---

[1] There is the peculiar and interesting case of Dr. John Byrom of Manchester. Some of his attractive poems are prosaic in the most obvious sense, being versified excerpts from the prose of William Law; while others are conversational in the sense that they appeal to spoken usage far from the discipline of even conversational prose. I know no other poet of the period in respect of whom it is feasible to make this distinction between conversational and prosaic diction.

[2] There have been poets, especially in recent years, who have done without some or all of the resources of logical syntax; and these poets have drawn upon very unstudied speech-usages, as far as possible from

between prosaic and conversational elements in poetic diction, is blurred from the start. Moreover, the eighteenth century is the age of great letter-writing, that is, of a form of writing which depends upon blurring the distinction between conversation and written prose. And so, to cut a long story short, it must appear that the 'common use' to which Johnson appeals is to be found in the letters written in his age.

This tie between the writing of poetry and the writing of letters makes it possible, and necessary, to speak of Johnson's diction as 'bourgeois'. On the one hand the poets under discussion often regarded themselves as spokesmen of the middle classes, which they valued as the most stable element in the commonwealth.[1] And on the other hand the great letters of the age were written by members of the bourgeoisie, in drawing-rooms like Mrs. Thrale's at Streatham. There is a notable difference between the letters of Mrs. Boscawen, for instance, and those of Lady Mary Wortley Montagu. Lady Mary's comments on *The Rambler* show her well aware of the difference between her age and Johnson's. For the difference between her letters and Mrs. Boscawen's is the same as that between *The Spectator* and *The Rambler*; Addison was a mannerly man and in that he was moral, Johnson was unmannerly but moral none the less. The 'common use' to which Prior appeals is in the letters of Lady Mary; the court

literary prose. John Byrom was one of these, and their work lies out of the present discussion. It seems just to speak of Johnson and Wordsworth, for example, as appealing to '*conversational*' usage, so long as we keep '*colloquial*' for the more daring usages exploited by these others.

[1] See, for instance, chapter xix of *The Vicar of Wakefield*; and cf. Hume's essay *On the Middle Station of Life*.

of appeal for Johnson is in Mrs. Thrale's letters, or Mrs. Boscawen's. People write of the diction of eighteenth-century poetry as if it were one thing, governing almost all writing from Dryden to Crabbe; and certainly Dryden, Johnson and Crabbe can be shown to draw upon a common stock of artifice and convention. But there is an important difference between the use of this common stock by Dryden, on the one hand, and Johnson on the other. We define this difference when we call Johnson's diction 'bourgeois' and 'pious'.

The two terms go together. For the culture of Prior, Lady Mary and Addison differed from that of Goldsmith, Mrs. Boscawen and Johnson, chiefly in this—that conversation and letters in the later period are far readier to discuss questions of personal conduct, not under cover of a code of manners, but directly, by appeal to the moral absolutes of Christian tradition.[1] This greater readiness appears also in the poetry. This Christianity of the later age is not so much a conviction, as a will to conviction; to a conviction which the poets can sometimes grasp, chiefly through sympathy with human sentiment, but which for the most part they can only desperately hope for and will into being. They seem to have no faculties for apprehending spiritual reality immediately, and in itself, but only as mediated in a struggling way through the natural and especially the human creation. This attitude I call 'pious', and it appears in their verse as a strenuous

[1] By Cowper's day this change in conversational habit was consciously advocated. See his poem "Conversation"; and cf. Mrs. Boscawen (Aspinall-Oglander, *Admiral's Wife* (Longmans, 1940), p. 34), for an example of the intimate letter moving easily into assured and quite complicated moral judgment.

determination to moralize the instance, making continual play with certain moral absolutes until each circumstance they write about can be lifted to a level of moral judgment and sympathy. Jane Austen called Cowper and Johnson 'her favourite moral writers'. We can hardly call them that; for we are likely to agree with Lady Mary that *Pamela* may do more harm than all the poems of Rochester; and Dr. Johnson's admiration of Richardson testifies, we may think, to a coarsening of the moral sense. What distinguishes him from Lady Mary is not a finer moral sense, but a more urgent moral concern. And it seems fair to call this his 'piety'.

We are saying that the poet who undertakes to preserve or refine a poetic diction is writing in a web of responsibilities. He is responsible to past masters for conserving the genres and the decorum which they have evolved. He is responsible to the persons or the themes on which he writes, to maintain a consistent tone and point of view in his dealings with them. He is responsible to the community in which he writes, for purifying and correcting the spoken language. And of course he is responsible, as all poets are, to his readers; he has to give them pleasure, and also, deviously or directly, instructions in proper conduct.

It follows that the poet who uses a diction must be very sure of the audience which he addresses. He dare not be merely the spokesman of their sentiments and habits, for he must purify the one and correct the other. Yet he dare not be quite at odds with his age, but must share with his readers certain assumptions. I am not sure if it matters how large or how small his audience is. Cowper in the last book of "The Task", like Wordsworth in his *Political Sonnets*, seems to address the whole English nation. Johnson and Goldsmith do not give this impression. On the other hand, none of these poets can have thought of himself as addressing only a coterie of personal friends and other poets, as most modern poets have to think. At this point, discussion of diction becomes discussion of the poet's place in the national community, or, under modern conditions (where true community exists only in pockets), his place in the state. This aspect of the matter will become clearer when we ask how the poet, in his choice of language, should be governed, if at all, by principles of taste. And this is inseparable from the question of what Goldsmith and others understood by chastity and propriety in language.

II

THE CHASTITY OF POETIC DICTION

Accordingto Goldsmith,[1] chastity in writing is the best safeguard against frigidity; and frigidity is "a deviation from propriety owing to the erroneous judgment of the writer, who, endeavouring to captivate the admiration with novelty, very often shocks the understanding with extravagance". This extravagance, he claims, betrays itself most often in the use of metaphor, and in two ways, in metaphors which are mixed and in metaphors which are laboured into conceits. It follows that hyperbolical and highly metaphorical language runs most risk of frigidity; and chastity therefore appears most often as restraint and economy in the use of metaphor.

Goldsmith allows that in certain genres the language may and should be less chaste than in others. Goldsmith gives no full account of the genres, and in practice he distinguishes only between the poetry of passion and the poetry of pathos. Chastity is more important in the poetry that aims at pathos:

Passion itself is very figurative, and often bursts out into metaphors; but, in touching the pathos, the poet must be perfectly well acquainted with the emotions of the human soul, and carefully distinguish between those metaphors which rise glowing

[1] I base this account of Goldsmith's doctrine on the three essays: "XV, Poetry distinguished from other writing"; "XVI, Metaphor"; and "XVII, Hyperbole". These essays are not very distinguished writing, and may be all the more representative of views commonly held by the readers of Goldsmith's age.

from the heart, and those cold conceits which are engendered in the fancy.

So Goldsmith can say:

The Ode and Satire admit of the boldest hyperboles: such exaggerations suit the impetuous warmth of the one; and, in the other, have a good effect in exposing folly, and exciting horror against vice.

The most important features, then, in this view of 'chastity' seem to be: first, that it is an effect attained through judgment and taste, not by imagination or passion or inspiration; second, that it is connected with sparing use of metaphor; and finally, that what is chaste in one genre may be flat in another.

When Goldsmith attempts to apply these principles, he can condemn a soliloquy from *Hamlet* on the score of mixed metaphor. But merely as principles they strike me as thoroughly sound; and Wordsworth's more famous discussion of diction seems weakest where it strays most from what Goldsmith lays down.

Wordsworth talks of 'chastity' in language, in the Appendix to his Preface, when he comments on two lines from Cowper:

> But the sound of the church-going bell
> These valleys and rocks never heard.

Wordsworth remarks:

The epithet 'church-going' applied to a bell, and that by so chaste a writer as Cowper, is an instance of the strange abuses which poets have introduced into their language, till they and their Readers take them as matter of course, if they do not single them out expressly as objects of admiration.

It seems as if 'chastity' meant much the same to Wordsworth and to Goldsmith. Wordsworth thinks an expression unchaste when it departs from the language of prose; Goldsmith thinks so when it departs from 'common use', the language of prose and careful conversation. One could even say that for both critics 'chastity' means, once again, economy in metaphor: for the discomfort we feel about Cowper's line derives from an unwanted metaphor, the ludicrous image of the bell itself trundling along the road to church. Of course the image is inadvertent, and of course we do not take it seriously; but it is present, and offensive, as we read.

Wordsworth's comments, on the two stanzas he quotes from Cowper, are very just. From them Wordsworth proceeds to lay down his principle:

—namely, that in works *of imagination and sentiment*, for of these only have I been treating, in proportion as ideas and feelings are valuable, whether the composition be in prose or in verse, they require and exact one and the same language.

From what we have said, it will appear that this formulation differs little from the warning of Goldsmith:

in touching the pathos, the poet must . . . carefully distinguish between those metaphors which rise glowing from the heart, and those cold conceits which are engendered in the fancy.

Where it differs, it differs for the worse; and chiefly in this—that what in Goldsmith was flexible, with Wordsworth is a rigid rule.[1]

[1] In practice, for instance, Wordsworth forgets the qualification in respect of the genre—"works *of imagination and sentiment*, for of these only have I been treating". The other example in this Appendix, Johnson's paraphrase of Proverbs vi, may be called a work of imagination (though not, perhaps, in any Wordsworthian sense), but it is hard to see by what stretch it can be described as a work of 'sentiment'. And I think that, in dismissing this admirable piece as 'a hubbub of words', Wordsworth is as flagrantly wrong as, on Cowper, he is plainly right.

THE CHASTITY OF POETIC DICTION

It is easy to see why Goldsmith could be flexible where Wordsworth could not. Goldsmith could confidently leave to his readers a margin for the exercise of judgment and taste. Wordsworth had no such confidence:

TASTE, I would remind the reader, like IMAGINATION, is a word which has been forced to extend its services far beyond the point to which philosophy would have confined them. It is a metaphor, taken from a *passive* sense of the human body, and transferred to things which are in their essence *not* passive,—to intellectual *acts* and *operations*. The word Imagination has been overstrained, from impulses honourable to mankind, to meet the demands of the faculty which is perhaps the noblest of our nature. In the instance of Taste, the process has been reversed; and from the prevalence of dispositions at once injurious and discreditable, being no other than that selfishness which is the child of apathy, —which, as Nations decline in productive and creative power, makes them value themselves upon a presumed refinement of judging. Poverty of language is the primary cause of the use which we make of the word Imagination; but the word Taste has been stretched to the sense which it bears in modern Europe by habits of self-conceit, inducing that inversion in the order of things whereby a passive faculty is made paramount among the faculties conversant with the fine arts. Proportion and congruity, the requisite knowledge being supposed, are subjects upon which taste may be trusted; it is competent to this office;—for in its intercourse with these the mind is *passive*, and is affected painfully or pleasurably as by an instinct. But the profound and the exquisite in feeling, the lofty and universal in thought and imagination; or, in ordinary language, the pathetic and the sublime;—are neither of them, accurately speaking, objects of a faculty which could ever without a sinking in the spirit of Nations have been designated by the metaphor—*Taste*. And Why? Because without the exertion of a co-operating *power* in the mind of the Reader, there can be no adequate sympathy with either of these emotions: without this auxiliary impulse, elevated or profound passion cannot exist.

Wordsworth here denies to taste any say in the choice of language, for the pathetic strain no less than the sublime. It is denied any authority on the plausible grounds that it is passive while the appreciation of pathos requires active co-operation from the reader. The argument from the metaphorical origin of the word 'taste' is telling; but like all arguments from origins, it cannot be conclusive. It is only Wordsworth who decides that the conception, taste, has remained true to its metaphorical origin as a passive faculty. Wordsworth, in fact, makes no distinction between 'taste' and 'fashion'.

Goldsmith holds by this distinction, and argues that taste is active, because informed by judgment. The acquisition and preservation of taste, according to Goldsmith, is a strenuous business:

> In order to restrain the luxuriancy of the young imagination, which is apt to run riot, to enlarge the stock of ideas, exercise the reason and ripen the judgment, the pupil must be engaged in the severer study of science. He must learn geometry, which Plato recommends for strengthening the mind, and enabling it to think with precision. He must be made acquainted with geography and chronology, and trace philosophy through all her branches. . . .

And so Goldsmith goes on, with a lifetime's regimen of study and discipline, all because "taste is a natural talent" only in origin, and "cannot be brought to perfection without proper cultivation; for taste pretends to judge, not only of nature, but also of art; and that judgment is founded upon observation and comparison".

At the risk of being shallow, we may say that for Wordsworth judgment in the poet was limited to the choice between going and not going to live in Cumberland. The rest was done by mountains and lakes and shepherds. He believed in a culture of the feelings, not in cultivation of taste. Taste, in art as in nature, was for him a province of feeling.

We should be naïve if we took this disagreement between Goldsmith and Wordsworth as a difference of philosophical opinion, about the hierarchy of human faculties. Neither of them has a philosopher's detachment. They differ because of the different conditions obtaining for each of them, as practising poets. Goldsmith could leave to taste and judgment a margin of activity in appreciating poetry; he could do so because he thought he found, among readers, a sufficient number whose taste and judgment seemed reliable. Wordsworth dare leave no margin of operation for taste and judgment; because he thought he found, among readers of poetry, only vicious taste and unstable judgment. Wordsworth had no such confidence in his readers as Goldsmith had in his. When he lost confidence in his public, the poet was thrown back upon confidence in himself. When this confidence, too, was shaken, it masked itself as hysterical arrogance. This is one way of describing the Romantic Revival.

Wordsworth, of course, found a half-way house. If he had lost confidence in the readers of London and Cambridge, he still had confidence in the readers of Cumberland and Somerset. In the same way, Jane Austen could still count upon the readers in rural rectories and small country-houses, though she had

lost confidence in the 'gad-about'[1] publics of London
and Bath and Brighton. As England transformed itself
into an industrial state, people were uprooted from
native localities and from the social and cultural disci-
plines of settled communities. Hence the importance,
for this literature, of the uprooted, nomadic and class-
less type of the governess and paid companion. Wordsworth and Jane Austen are trying to hand on, to these
new types, the values of the older society. Edmund
Bertram is educating the typical *déracinée*, Fanny Price,
in the values of that rooted life which has been denied
her. And the eldest of "The Brothers", in Wordsworth's poem of that name, having broken from the
community, is unable to return to it, and has to be
instructed anew by the natural spokesman of the community, the village pastor. The case of Jane Austen is
particularly clear, for to a reader conversant with "The
Task", Jane Austen appears to appeal continually to
Cowper, for a standard of the older kind by which to
judge the conduct of her characters. These references
are so closely veiled that they are missed by anyone
who knows Cowper less well than Jane Austen's family
knew him. Cowper constitutes, in fact, that 'moral

[1] I think that when Jane Austen allows a character to be described
as 'a gad', she is embarking upon a question important for her, and
putting a question-mark against the moral stability of that character.
Sanditon, the fragmentary last novel, seems particularly concerned with
this question, and I cannot agree with Mr. E. M. Forster about it, but
think that, if it had been completed, it might have been one of Jane
Austen's most interesting and important books. The rise of the seaside
resort—Brighton, Worthing, Scarborough—was one of the most
marked and significant social changes of Wordsworth's and Jane
Austen's period. Cobbett shows himself concerned with it and sus-
picious of it; and there is a mildly satirical poem by Robert Bloomfield
about Worthing.

positive', which is so elusive in Jane Austen's work, which so many of her readers have missed and joyfully gone without. From one point of view, Wordsworth stands with her, for the sobriety of Goldsmith and Cowper, against the 'glare and glitter' of Gray and Beattie and Logan, the poets of the uprooted.

Only in this way can one explain why no considerable poet since Goldsmith and Cowper has taken, as a guide to his writing, the good sense of 'the best people'. The centre fell apart. In architecture and furnishing, as in literature, the people with the money to command the best began to command something else; and taste and judgment no longer went with power and wealth. Inferior art, such as the 'tales of terror', satisfied the depraved taste of the wealthy, the leisured and the eminent; and whereas, fifty years before, bad architecture and poetry had been dull, now they were vulgar. Because the poets could no longer trust the taste of their readers, they could be guided no longer, in their choice of language, by the conversational usages of those readers. In any case, that conversation must have deteriorated; for the literary forms which depended upon it, the familiar letter and the epistolary novel, fell suddenly below the level of serious art. It is not fantastic to surmise that Jane Austen in England, and Pushkin in Russia, first realized the social break-up when they tried to write the epistolary novel, and failed. With the stay of 'common use' thus taken away, the notions of chastity and purity in diction could have no meaning. Wordsworth tried to preserve the meaning by anchoring it to a hard-and-fast principle. But Coleridge showed that this was impracticable; and so the diction of the Romantic poets is extremely impure. Keats is a flagrant case—in all but his best work, his language oscillates wildly between a colloquialism which is slang and a literary pomp which is exotic; and his own ideas about 'purity' were puerile.[1] Byron in "Don Juan", like Mr. Auden in our own day, found an ingenious solution in deliberately causing such oscillations, exploiting a sort of calculated impurity. As it happened, most of the Romantic poets affected the sublime rather than the pathetic; so that the impurity of their diction, though still a discomfort when one has learnt to love chastity, does not matter so much. But it must be said that, of all the nineteenth-century poets since Wordsworth, none has 'purified the language of the tribe'. They have enriched that language, and with some of them, such as Hopkins, the enrichment is so great that we can feel the question of purity impertinent; but the spoken tongue has suffered at their hands.

The critic who most nearly recognized the loss was Matthew Arnold, when he lamented the absence, from English writing, of 'the tone of the centre'. The argument is to be found in "The Literary Influence of Academies"; and what is there said of 'Attic' prose, its value and its significance, seems to me equally applicable to chaste diction in poetry. A chaste diction is 'central', in Arnold's sense; it expresses the feeling of

[1] "The purest English I think—or what ought to be the purest—is Chatterton's. The Language had existed long enough to be entirely uncorrupted of Chaucer's gallicisms and still the old words are used. Chatterton's language is entirely northern." Keats confuses diction with language. Chatterton employed a very eccentric and impure diction. One can speak of pure and impure diction. To speak of pure or impure *language* is as ridiculous as it is to speak of a pure or impure *tree*.

the capital, not the provinces. And it can do this because it is central in another way, central to the language,
conversational not colloquial, poetic not poetical. The
effect is a valuable urbanity, a civilized moderation and
elegance; and this is the effect attainable, as I think,
by Goldsmith, and not by Shakespeare. It seemed to
Arnold that this matter was the responsibility of prose-
writers, something from which the poets could be
absolved: and all critics have agreed,[1] until Mr. Eliot
asserted that "to have the virtues of good prose is the
first and minimum requirement of great poetry".[2] This

[1] A good statement, of a position close to Arnold's, is made by J. S.
Phillimore—"Poetry is a wind that bloweth where it listeth: a barbaric
people may have great poetry, they cannot have great prose. Prose is an
institution, part of the equipment of a civilization, part of its heritable
wealth, like its laws, or its system of schooling, or its tradition of skilled
craftsmanship." *Dublin Review*, vol. cliii (1913), p. 8. Quoted by
R. W. Chambers, *The Continuity of English Prose from Alfred to More
and his School* (Oxford, 1932).

[2] One has to agree with Dr. Leavis (*Revaluation*, p. 122) that the
poetry of "Ash Wednesday" has not 'the virtues of good prose'. But it
is common for poets to know the way they ought to go before they can
follow their own advice. And an apter example of Mr. Eliot practising
what he preaches comes from "Little Gidding":

> "There are three conditions which often look alike
> Yet differ completely, flourish in the same hedge-row:
> Attachment to self and to things and to persons, detachment
> From self and from things and from persons; and, growing
> between them, indifference
> Which resembles the others as death resembles life,
> Being between two lives—unflowering, between
> The live and the dead nettle. This is the use of memory;
> For liberation—not less of love, but expanding
> Of love beyond desire, and so liberation
> From the future as well as the past."

"Ash Wednesday" is a poem in the symbolist tradition. Images or
symbols are ranged about, and the meaning flowers out of the space
between them. Poetry of this sort depends upon the dislocation of
normal syntax, and so it can never be written in a pure diction. It seems

comment must be taken along with the same critic's contempt of those persons "who cannot understand that it is more important, in some vital respects, to be a *good* poet than to be a *great* poet". And in the rest of this book I shall be concerned with poets who are 'good', rather than 'great', to show how their work has the virtues of good prose and yet is good poetry. I shall think that their poems have the virtues of prose if I can establish that their diction is chaste; and I shall think them good poetry if I can show that, when necessary, they have the metaphorical richness and force we associate with poetry of quite another sort.

to me that the most enduring work of both W. B. Yeats and T. S. Eliot is that in which they have reached a pure diction. For the other (Shakespearean) kind of verse-writing in our age we have to go to some prolific and unequal poets of America, Hart Crane, Wallace Stevens and Allen Tate. The best poetry of Yeats and Eliot has the virtues of good prose; the best poetry of Crane, Tate and Stevens has not. On the other hand minor modern poets on both sides of the Atlantic have employed successfully for their limited ends a personal diction deliberately impure, eccentric and mannered. Robert Graves, Marianne Moore and John Crowe Ransom are examples. To compare Eliot's verse above with Yeats' "Prayer for My Daughter" is to see how two poems can be equally chaste, while differing widely in tone; Yeats is lofty, Eliot is what Puttenham would call 'mean'.

III

THE LANGUAGE OF THE TRIBE

(i) *Live and Dead Metaphors*

T H E best account of metaphor known to me is a fine and subtle essay by Owen Barfield.[1] Mr. Barfield remarks that simile, metaphor and symbol are all devices for seeming to say one thing (B) while really saying another (A). This process is called in German '*Tarnung*', anglicized by Mr. Barfield as 'tarning'; and it is essential not to poetic language alone but to all language. For the greater part of any language consists of so-called 'dead' metaphors, that is, of words produced by tarning, but so long ago that they are used with no consciousness of the tarning behind them. Something similar occurs in law. For instance, the sort of tarning known as 'personification' corresponds to "the personification of limited companies by which they are enabled to sue and be sued at law". A more complicated tarning in law produces the fictitious characters, John Doe and Richard Roe. This is now a sort of dead metaphor in the courts; but when the device was first introduced 'John Doe' was a live metaphor. And so—

The long analogy which I have been drawing may be expressed more briefly in the formula—metaphor: language: meaning:: legal fiction: law: civil life.[2]

[1] Owen Barfield, "Poetic Diction and Legal Fiction", in *Essays Presented to Charles Williams* (Oxford, 1947).
[2] *Ibid.* p. 121.

For just as law is consistent, inflexible and determinate, yet must, to keep pace with social changes, have recourse to fictions; so language is fixed and determinate, to satisfy needs of logic, yet must, to keep pace with changes in thought and life, evolve new meanings by way of metaphor.

Mr. Barfield finds a neat example in Bacon (*Novum Organum*, iii, 2), where the writer seeks to define the notion now familiar as the dead metaphor, the 'laws of nature'; Bacon tries by simile to appropriate to this signification the word 'forma', the Platonic 'form', and it is only in a casual metaphor that he produces the word 'lex'. But the casual metaphor was adopted. It is a dead metaphor now; yet it can come to embarrassing and dangerous life. For that reason we have to be aware, or be made aware, of the force still latent in metaphors that sham dead.

Most interesting in the present connection is an observation which Mr. Barfield does not care to develop. After dealing with figurative language, he remarks:

> I do not say that these particular methods of expression are an absolute *sine qua non* of poetic diction. They are not. Poetry may also take the form of simple and literal statement. But figurative expression is found everywhere; its roots descend very deep, as we shall see, into the nature, not only of poetry, but of language itself. If you take away from the stream of European poetry every passage of a metaphorical nature, you would reduce it to a very thin trickle indeed, pure though the remainder beverage might be to the taste. Perhaps our English poetry would suffer the heaviest damage of all.[1]

Is this the purity of which we speak when we talk of 'a

[1] Owen Barfield, *loc. cit.* p. 107.

pure diction'? It may be, since many critics were seen to agree in making economy in metaphor a feature of pure diction. But, as Mr. Barfield points out, almost all language is metaphorical at bottom. It would be hard, perhaps impossible, to find a poem in English where the literal statement is completely unmetaphorical. And so, when we say of a pure diction that it has few passages of a metaphorical nature, we must be supposed to speak only of metaphors which are *overt*. It would, therefore, be almost true to say that the poet who employs a diction chooses to include only metaphors that are dead. This would seem to condemn such poetry. But it need not do so. For such poetry, by exploiting 'rhythm, sound, music' (elements which Mr. Barfield deliberately excludes from his study), may revivify metaphors gone dead. It could be agreed, for instance, that the personifications of Pope are newly minted and live metaphors: and if it could be proved that Johnson limited himself for the most part to the personifications of Pope (metaphors gone dead in the hands of Pope's imitators), it could be argued that Johnson, by his different use, brought these metaphors to life again. If so, this would be the poetry which attempts, in Mr. Eliot's phrase, to 'purify the language of the tribe'. For if the poet who coins new metaphors *enlarges* the language, the poet who enlivens dead metaphors can be said to *purify* the language.

As Mr. Barfield says, this kind of poetry is rare in English. And we must beware of thinking we find it when we do not. Crabbe describes Chaucer as one of "those who address their productions to the plain sense and sober judgment of their readers, rather than to their fancy and imagination"; and we certainly do not think of Chaucer as a highly metaphorical poet. But of course Chaucer's poems are not examples of chaste diction. Chaucer is, more than Pope, an original, revolutionary poet, expanding the language, creating metaphors, and creating, through them, new areas of meaning. We should look for a poet who stands, in relation to Chaucer, much as Johnson stands to Pope; and it is in Gower that we find a chaste diction.[1]

If the function of pure diction in poetry is to purify the language by revivifying dead metaphor, we shall look for purity of diction in writing at the end of a strong tradition. This explains why we have recourse to the term in respect of Johnson, Goldsmith, Collins and Cowper, poets writing more or less completely in the Augustan tradition, and late in that tradition. But not only the language of previous poetry can provide dead metaphors: they appear no less in conversation and in prose. Hence pure diction can be found where a poet has tried to revivify the dead metaphors of studied conversation or artless prose. Indeed, who that has read the letters of Mrs. Boscawen or Mrs. Thrale could affirm that Johnson's personifications, or Cowper's, do not derive from letters or conversation rather than the *Essay on Man* or Shaftesbury's *Characteristics*? Because eighteenth-century prose was conversational, it is idle to debate whether the diction of a poem of that period is conversational or prosaic.[2] So, in the case

---

[1] Cf. C. S. Lewis, *The Allegory of Love*, p. 201.

[2] C. S. Lewis, however, can not only define the diction of Gower as conversational rather than prosaic, but can specify the *sort* of conversation, common to what classes and in what conditions.

of a modern 'prosaic' poem like Karl Shapiro's "Essay on Rime", the poet's intention can be defined as 'an advance of one degree in shapeliness of statement';[1] but one cannot say whether it is an advance on conversation or on prose.

In any case what is important is the source of that impulse towards shapeliness, in Gower and Johnson and Shapiro alike. This tug away from 'common use' can come only from art, from the usages of previous literature. Thus it appears that a pure diction is governed by two sorts of precedent, on the one hand the usages of previous poets, on the other hand the usages of polite conversation. These were just the standards to which, in the beginning of this discussion, we saw Johnson appealing, when he criticized a locution of Gray. In the case of Johnson himself, the literary precedent was usually Dryden, and through him the poets of Rome; and the conversational precedent was Mrs. Thrale's drawing-room. The dead metaphors of poetry are brought to life by the tang of common usage; and vice versa.

(ii) *Enlivened Metaphors*

On Owen Barfield's showing, metaphor is an extension of areas of meaning; and poets who use a diction engage themselves not to extend meaning, but to work over areas already explored. Their principal object is the re-creation of metaphors which have ossified into meanings, rubbed smooth by too much handling.

[1] I am indebted for this accurate formulation to my friend Douglas Brown.

The crassest example of this is the Latinate pun, as found in three examples which Mr. John Arthos takes from Dryden:

> . . . the morning dew prevents the sun . . .;
> . . . horrid with fern . . .;
> . . . with steel invades his brother's life . . .[1]

If we are to use the language with circumspection, it is good for us to be reminded of the metaphor embalmed in the word 'horrid', the image of hair standing up on the observer's head. Even in Dryden's time, however, this diction must have been unchaste, for these expressions are too far from conversational usage. In other words, the metaphor is not really re-created at all. There is too wide a gap between the 'horrid' of common use and the 'horrid' of scholarly use, for the metaphorical spark to leap across. And this is true of most, not all, of such puns.

A different but still crude example comes from "The Deserted Village":

> O luxury! thou cursed by heaven's decree,
> How ill exchanged are things like these for thee!
> How do thy potions, with insidious joy,
> Diffuse their pleasures only to destroy!
> Kingdoms by thee, to sickly greatness grown,
> Boast of a florid vigour not their own:
> At every draught more large and large they grow,
> A bloated mass of rank unwieldy woe;
> Till sapp'd their strength, and every part unsound,
> Down, down they sink, and spread a ruin round.

[1] John Arthos, *The Language of Natural Description in Eighteenth Century Poetry* (University of Michigan Press, 1949).

This is an attempt to revivify the dead metaphor of 'the body politic', the metaphor which Burke spent his time bringing to life; and it is most nearly successful with the prosaic epithet 'florid'.

More subtle and remarkable are Shenstone's beautiful lines:

> So first when Phoebus met the Cyprian queen,
> And favour'd Rhodes beheld their passion crown'd,
> Unusual flowers enrich'd the painted green,
> And swift spontaneous roses blush'd around.

The image comes out of common poetic stock.[1] Shenstone refreshes it. It is just as logical to describe the flowers as unusual, swift and spontaneous as it is to describe their flowering in those terms. But because we had thought of these as features of the event, not of its effects, Shenstone presses upon our notice the logic of his transference of these terms to the roses. The logic of the usage being thus impressed upon us, these words strike us as dry and prosaic; and they have the effect of a taunting gravity and sobriety which chastens the reader as it pleases him.

Moreover, by taking adverbs and turning them into other parts of speech, the poet leaves the verb singularly naked and powerful. Probably there was something in the metrical exigencies of the couplet which demanded that the verb should beat so sharply into the

---

[1] Cf., for instance, Sir John Suckling, "Upon my Lady Carlisle's walking in Hampton Court Gardens":

> "Didst thou not find the place inspired,
> And flowers as if they had desired
> No other sun, start from their beds,
> And for a sight steal out their heads?"

35

line, pinning it and making it quiver. At any rate it is true that the best eighteenth-century verse strikes us as active and weighty, governed by the forceful verb. We do not remember this when we censure this verse for luxuriance of epithets. The poets themselves censured it on the same grounds; and of course it is true that this luxuriance is the bane of the poor poetry of the period. But where it appears in the good poets, it is often the condition of an unusual metaphorical force residing in the verb. This can be seen, to begin with, simply in accurate register of appearances:

> Urging at noon the slow boat in the reeds
> That wav'd their green uncertainty of shade. (Langhorne)

Here 'urging', naked and conspicuous because 'slow' has been removed (at no expense to logic) to qualify 'boat', comes over with all the force of muscular exertion. 'Wav'd', too, profits from being left alone; and 'uncertainty' is dry, prosaic and chastening. So again, Goldsmith:

> No more thy glassy brook reflects the day,
> But choked with sedges works its weedy way

—where 'works' takes all the thrust of the meaning and bears along the clutter of epithets. The same thing occurs when the theme is more abstract:

> The bold Bavarian, in a luckless hour,
> Tries the dread summits of Caesarian pow'r,
> With unexpected legions bursts away,
> And sees defenceless realms receive his sway;

The metaphor submerged in the expression 'rebellion

broke out' comes, in Johnson's hands, to violent life. 'Breaks' becomes 'bursts', and strikes out, naked and powerful, because the unexpectedness of the outbreak has been transferred to the instrument, the legions. 'Unexpected', as applied to the legions, seems prosaic and grave, yet taunting in its moderation—"There's no need to get so excited". Once the trick has been noticed, one finds it everywhere. It can even work through and over a whole poem. This is the case, for instance, with Gray's "Impromptu", where the stock image (corrupt politicians = foxes) comes to shocking life[1] in the last line:

> Owls would have hooted in St. Peter's choir
> And foxes stunk and littered in St. Paul's.

The metaphor comes to life because the force of it has shifted on to the verbs, those magnificently 'foxy' verbs, 'stunk' and 'littered', both coming straight out of speech.

This is a poetry of energy, of force and momentum. This is especially true of Johnson, much truer of him, I think, than of Charles Churchill, who is frequently singled out of this period for his 'energy'. Johnson's verse trembles over our heads, like a thin ceiling shaken by a heavy tread:

> For such the steady Romans shook the world.

Sound echoes sense, and the verse *is* what it says. Dr. Leavis shows how dead metaphors are brought to life

[1] This poem seems to me, together with the fragmentary "Education and Government", and (in the main) the "Elegy", the only writings of Gray in which the diction is chaste in Johnson's sense or any other. The effect of Gray's example (e.g. in his Odes) was decadent and disruptive; and I can find little of value in his other poems.

37

when he remarks finely (*Revaluation*, p. 118), "That 'steady' turns the vague *cliché*, 'shook the world', into the felt percussion of tramping legions". It is the tread that is steady, but we are shaken by it only when the steadiness is transferred to the Romans.[1]

(iii) *Personification*

This habit of throwing metaphorical force from noun to verb produces personification. For it must seem that an abstraction is personified to some extent as soon as it can govern an active verb:

> When fainting nature call'd for aid,
>> And hovering death prepar'd the blow,
> His vigorous remedy display'd
>> The power of art without the show.

Here, surely, 'nature', 'death' and 'remedy' are all, somehow, personified. But 'remedy' is less abstract than 'nature' or 'death'; and 'calling' and 'preparing' are associated, more often than 'displaying', with a personal agent. Hence we have to say that 'remedy' is personified hardly at all; just as in Cowper's line,

> Obscurest night involv'd the sky

—the verb 'involv'd' is so remote from human action

---

[1] I have been puzzled by Dr. Leavis' description of Johnson as 'weighty'. Not that I would disagree; but I cannot decide whether the critic is aware of his own puns. For instance, he quotes:

> "For why did Wolsey near the steeps of fate,
>> On weak foundations raise th' enormous weight?"

And I find something comical in the comment: "The effect of that is massive; the images are both generalized, and unevadably concrete". Must I think that Dr. Leavis is being impish?

that 'night' can hardly be said to be personified. This may seem to be a quibble, but without it we are at a loss to detect personification except by a capital letter.

What matters is the extent to which personification can be truly metaphorical; and on this showing the extent to which it can be metaphorical depends upon the verb it governs:

> Then with no fiery, throbbing pain,
>   No cold gradations of decay,
> Death broke at once the vital chain,
>   And freed his soul the nearest way.

The verb 'broke', reaping the cumulative interest and movement of the first two lines, enlivens alike the personification which governs it and the dead metaphor ('the vital chain') which follows. And the effect is reinforced by the conversational looseness of the final line.

The true personification, the one with the force of metaphor, is often left, in this way, until the last lines. This is the case, for instance, with that paraphrase of Proverbs, which Wordsworth thought beneath contempt:

> Till Want now following, fraudulent and slow,
>   Shall spring to seize thee, like an ambush'd foe.

The process of beggary is gradual, yet indigence comes on a sudden. Johnson's 'spring' is faithful to this painful paradox, as true to his Scripture as to the human experience of the Bankruptcy Court. And the method is the one we have analyzed, stripping the action of adverbs ('deceitfully', 'slowly') and transferring the sense of them to the personified agent, making them

prosaic and logical, with a sobering ring, like the fine
'fraudulent'.[1]

(iv) *Generalization*

Another sort of personification in these poets comes
with the habit of generalizing. This habit has been
accounted for in three ways. In the first place, we are
invited to consider an analogy with the visual arts, and
remember how Reynolds, for instance, insisted that
beauty resided only in the general and typical. Then,

[1] This seems to me the most important sort of personification, the
most capable of exerting metaphorical force. There is another sort,
which will be recalled more readily. This is the allegorical set-piece:

> "O vale of bliss! O softly swelling hills!
> On which the power of cultivation lies,
> And joys to see the wonders of his toil."

Goldsmith comments on these lines: "We cannot conceive a more
beautiful image than that of the Genius of Agriculture, distinguished
by the implements of his art, imbrowned with labour, glowing with
health, crowned with a garland of foliage, flowers, and fruit, lying
stretched at his ease on the brow of a gently swelling hill, and con-
templating with pleasure the happy effects of his own industry". We
cannot deny that there is beauty in the picture visualized by Goldsmith, and though he contributes much that is unsaid by Thomson, he
probably contributes nothing that was not in Thomson's intention.
For Thomson could count on finding in his readers a ready allegorical
imagination, such as seems lost to us to-day. The loss is certainly ours.
A symptom and, it may be, a cause of this allegorical sense was the
popularity of the allegorical history-painting in the style of Thornhill.
We probably mistake the joke in chapter xvi of *The Vicar of Wakefield*
if we find it ridiculous that Mrs. Primrose should wish to be painted
as Venus. The absurdity lies rather in the refusal of the rest of the
group to be painted in roles in keeping with hers. On the other hand
this was the practice which led Goldsmith to suppose that all imagery
was pictorial (a supposition elevated into absurd principle by Erasmus
Darwin later). And in any case this sort of personification has little or
nothing to do with language, and is found most often in the dissident
or decadent poets of the period, poets whose diction was, for better or
worse, impure.

there are critics (usually adverse) who remind us of the obtrusive moral concern of these poets, their didacticism which made them push on to draw their moral without waiting to see things 'in themselves'. And finally we are asked to notice (and to deplore) how these poets confounded their function with that of the scientists,[1] looking always for the laws governing experience, and (again) careless of the thing in itself.

All three of these explanations are true, yet none is wholly true in itself. For instance, it is easy to point out, when we rise from reading Reynolds, how Johnson's elegy on Robert Levett is also 'the character of a good physician', so that we mourn in the poem not the death of a man, but the mortality of a profession; or how Goldsmith's elegy on Thomas Parnell is, in the same way, the character of a good poet. But Pope, too, through the eyes of a moralist, thought man should be classified under types. And when he wrote that "the proper study of mankind is man", he seems to have meant that men were objects of study as flowers were for botanists—his own theory of the ruling passions is a pseudo-scientific classification of human behaviour. Again, all Christians in the eighteenth century were natural theologians. It was not only deists who thought the nature of God could be seen in His Creation; everybody thought so, and nearly everybody thought that He could be deduced by tracing laws and classes, not

---

[1] Johnson's comment on lines from Dryden's "Annus Mirabilis"— "It had better become Dryden's learning and genius to have laboured science into poetry, and have shewn, by explaining longitude, that verse did not refuse the ideas of philosophy". The science of marine navigation was laboured into poetry, soon after Johnson wrote, by Falconer in "The Shipwreck".

perceived in a leap of insight. The poets were anxious to prove this in their verses. It is impossible, therefore, to decide whether the poets, in generalizing, were governed by aesthetic or moral or scientific principle. Probably it would not have occurred to them to make these distinctions. Moralist and poet and scientist and painter thought confidently that they were moving to the same point from different directions. Reynolds and Pope and Newton are at one.

The workings of the scientific principle are especially interesting:

> It may very well be that many poets accepted the idea of a conventional language for poetry because they considered the interests of poetry and natural philosophy to be the same in many important respects. Scientific writing required a set vocabulary according to set principles, and it must therefore follow that poetry's needs were similar. This is the extreme conclusion. It is, of course, truer of some poets than of others. But its general validity seems proved by the fact that so many of the same terms are found in scientific prose and in the poetry of the eighteenth century.[1]

When Wordsworth asserted that there is no essential difference between the language of prose and that of poetry, he seemed to think that his principle was revolutionary. And we have taken him at his own valuation ever since. But John Arthos establishes that, for instance, the adjectives formed by the -y suffix ('beamy', 'moony', 'sluicy'), words we have thought eminently false-poetical, are to be found frequently in scientific writing of the seventeenth and eighteenth centuries. It seems, then, that the language of eigh-

[1] John Arthos, *The Language of Natural Description in Eighteenth Century Poetry* (University of Michigan Press, 1949), p. 88.

teenth-century poetry is close to prose even when it seems most remote. Wordsworth's contention therefore was not revolutionary at all.[1]

Of course all this is historical explanation. It explains why poets adopted such language as they did; it does not justify their doing so. We justify them when we can show how, in the best of them, this language became poetic; and for the moment we can continue to suppose language poetic when it is deeply and seriously metaphorical. I propose to show how the generalizing habit can produce poignant and memorable metaphor.

This habit can be seen at work on all the parts of speech. The most obvious sort of generalized noun, for instance, is 'grove', as used by eighteenth-century poets to denote all assemblies of trees, or 'gale' as used to denote all movements of air. Often these usages offend the modern reader. He is aware of niceties of discrimination represented by 'thicket', 'wood', 'forest', 'copse', 'clump', 'brushwood', 'spinney'; or by 'squall', 'breeze', 'hurricane', 'whirlwind', 'gust', 'breath', 'wind'. And the eighteenth-century poets, by ignoring these words, seem culpably to miss so many chances of seeing the world more nearly. But a grove is planted, and to see all groups of trees as groves is to see them all in the park of a creator-god. Hence this generalization implies a view of the natural creation as a divinely ordered hierarchy. In the same way, to see a breeze and a hurricane

---

[1] Of course the language of eighteenth-century natural philosophy was not, like scientific language to-day, dry and colourless. It was figurative and excited. We can note how Berkeley's prose becomes most metaphorical and 'poetic' when most scientific, in "Siris". See my "Berkeley's Style in 'Siris' ", *Cambridge Journal*, vol. iv, no. 7.

alike as 'gales' is to come so much nearer seeing all movements of air as breathings from the mouth of God. In modern critical parlance, to describe an image as 'specific' is to approve it; but it is important to remember that an image can be more specific, and in one sense less exact.

Another sort of generalized name, just the same in principle, is used by these poets to describe the phenomena of human behaviour and feeling. These again are personifications, personified passions such as Scorn, Anger, Envy, Sloth, and personified moral principles, Honour, Charity, Virtue, Tolerance. These words cause the modern reader the same discomfort as words like 'grove'. For he is conditioned by his reading of the European novel, reading which has instructed him how many different histories and processes, what different sorts of attitude and outlook, are herded under the one blanketing term, 'Envy', or 'Shame', or 'Anger'; and, again, what different sorts of behaviour must, at a push, be approved alike as 'virtue' or condemned alike as 'vice'.[1] But Johnson or Goldsmith was not concerned with those features which make a man unique, but with those which he has in common with his fellows. The two sorts of concern are different though not incompatible; but there are no *a priori*

[1] The way the novel gets between us and eighteenth-century poetry is exemplified by John Crowe Ransom (*Kenyon Review*, xii, 3, 504), where, speaking of the good prose which Wordsworth liked, he says, "It would not be the merely utilitarian prose, but the prose to be found in sermons, in literary essays, above all in our time in prose fiction, and wherever else the style develops the concretions of nature rather than the lean 'concretions of discourse' ". This was not the prose our poets esteemed, and their achievement is in concretions of discourse, like personifications.

grounds for thinking one less interesting or less moral than the other.

The sort of interest one can expect from the generalizing habit, when it works in this way, can be seen in Johnson's Prologue to "A Word to the Wise":[1]

> This night presents a play which public rage,
> Or right, or wrong, once hooted from the stage.
> From zeal or malice, now no more we dread,
> For English vengeance wars not with the dead.
> A generous foe regards with pitying eye
> The man whom fate has laid where all must lie.
> To wit reviving from its author's dust,
> Be kind, ye judges, or at least be just,
> For no renew'd hostilities invade
> The oblivious grave's inviolable shade.
> Let one great payment every claim appease,
> And him, who cannot hurt, allow to please;
> To please by scenes unconscious of offence,
> By harmless merriment or useful sense.
> Where aught of bright, or fair, the piece displays,
> Approve it only—'tis too late to praise.
> If want of skill, or want of care appear,
> Forbear to hiss—the poet cannot hear.
> By all, like him, must praise and blame be found,
> At best a fleeting gleam, or empty sound.
> Yet then shall calm reflection bless the night,
> When liberal pity dignify'd delight;
> When pleasure fired her torch at Virtue's flame,
> And Mirth was Bounty with an humbler name.

The sudden cluster of capital letters, in the last two lines of this poem, is no accident. The words thus dignified—Virtue, Mirth, Bounty—are personified moral principles of the sort to which we have objected,

[1] I should like to acknowledge that I was first directed to this admirable poem by Mr. Yvor Winters.

on the score that they ignore the many and baffling ways in which they exert and display themselves in the world. But it is plain that this aspect of their activity is not disregarded by Johnson. They come at the end of the poem because they have been worked for in the rest. They struggle into the light, under pressure from the poet, through the brakes and tangles of human behaviour. Johnson brings home to the audience of a second-rate play by a dead author, the truth that their reception of the play involves a moral decision on their part and lays them open to moral judgment by others. A response which appears in the first lines as 'no more than common decency' ('For English vengeance wars not with the dead') has become, by the end, a moral judgment appealing to moral absolutes. And the judgment shrugged aside at first, in respect of the first performance—'or right, or wrong'—is inflexibly applied to the play's revival. If the reader looks back, from the vantage-point of the last couplet, he sees how earlier lines which pretend to finality of judgment (by their epigrammatic balance), are in fact only partial resolutions and intermediate stages. Thus:

> To wit reviving from its author's dust,
> Be kind, ye judges, or at least be just . . .

The pronouncement has a memorable neatness. But by the end of the poem Johnson has shown that to be kind is the only way of being just, in the given set of circumstances. Personifications and generalizations are justifiable according as they are 'worked for'.[1] If Johnson had

[1] Cf. 'custom' and 'ceremony' at the end of Yeats' "Prayer for My Daughter". They have been worked for like Johnson's 'Mirth' and 'Bounty'; and could sustain capital letters no less imperturbably.

concluded his poem with 'Be kind, ye judges, or at least be just', or with 'By harmless merriment or useful sense', the poem would have been trivial. And for merriment or sense to take capital letters would have been more than the poem could bear. As it is, a dead metaphor comes to life; Bounty is plenitude and *bonté* (goodness). Mirth is thankful enjoyment of the plenitude of creative providence; it is a compelling and dignified idea.

The case of the epithet is more complicated. It is the function of an epithet to define more nearly the thing to which it refers. One can hardly speak, therefore, of *generalizing* epithets. Yet the characteristic epithets of eighteenth-century poetry have a generalizing effect, for they specify only to the extent that they place a thing in its appropriate class, or assign it its appropriate function. Mr. Arthos makes an interesting suggestion to this effect,[1] when he compares the habitual coupling of one epithet with one noun, with the Linnaean system of classification in botany. Probably the epithets in -*y* ('beamy', 'moony' and the rest) were adopted from science for the same purpose of classification. These are not really adjectival in their form or their effect, but nouns only disguised by the termination. Other epithets, as we saw with Shenstone's 'swift spontaneous roses', are really disguised adverbs. And others again are verbs in their participial form—'the pleasing strain', 'the smiling land'.

Of course, if we say that the epithets of this verse describe a thing only by giving it its place in a system or its function in a scheme, we speak only of their

[1] Arthos, *op. cit.* p. 41.

original purpose in the hands of the best poets. Bryant, for instance, addresses the waterfowl:

> Seek'st thou the plashy brink
> Of weedy lake or marge of river wide,
> Or where the rocking billows rise and sink
> On the chaf'd ocean-side?

Bryant here is moralizing the instance, and arguing from the waterfowl to God, quite in the way of Johnson or Cowper. But he came into contact with that English tradition largely through his reading of Blair and Kirke White, poets in whom the characteristic diction had become corrupt. This corruption usually took a Miltonic or a Spenserian form. This is the impurity in 'plashy'. 'Weedy', however, is strong and chaste; for bulrushes are weeds, and to call them so shuts out Sabrina and Midas and their whispering, placing them firmly in the vegetable Kingdom where, for this poet as for the botanist, they belong. In using the word, Bryant has already taken one step away from the specific instance towards the divine law which governs it.

What is common to all these epithets is the way they turn their back upon sense-experience and appeal beyond it, logically, to known truths deduced from it.[1]

[1] There is an interesting example of the dry and abstract prosaic epithet in Wordsworth's "The Brothers":

> "and, when the regular wind
> Between the tropics filled the steady sail".

But Wordsworth does not know what to do with this felicity, and blunts it by repeating himself:

> "And blew with the same breath through days and weeks,
> Lengthening invisibly its weary line
> Along the cloudless main. . . ."

This is redundant and prolix.

It is always possible, by a discreet extravagance, to widen this gap between the evidence of the senses and the evidence deduced from them, until the image seems absurd while we know it to be true. This is one of the sources of the mock-heroic, which is therefore a possibility inherent in this sort of diction. One obvious way of widening the gap is to invade the world of the microscope:

> Fair insect! that, with threadlike legs spread out
>   And blood-extracting bill and filmy wing,
> Dost murmur, as thou slowly sail'st about,
>   In pitiless ears full many a plaintive thing,
> And tell how little our large veins should bleed
> Would we but yield them to thy bitter need;—

The 'threadlike legs' of the mosquito, his 'blood-extracting bill' and 'filmy wing', are known facts deduced from experience. But they cannot be said to agree with experience. For the mosquito, thus described, appears grotesque and comical,[1] because, in our experience, the smallness of the insect prevents us from noting these features. This union of the comical and the grotesque can be made horrific:

---

[1] Bryant's verse is not wholly successful. Comical and grotesque it is, but I think he meant it to be pathetic too. This union of the comic, the grotesque and the pathetic is achieved by Parnell:

> "Where stands a slender Fern's aspiring Shade,
> Whose answ'ring Branches regularly lay'd
> Put forth their answ'ring Boughs, and proudly rise
> Three stories upward, in the nether skies."

It belies the evidence of the senses to call the stalk and stems of a fern 'branches' and 'boughs', which we think of as massive. Yet, logically, that is what they are. The pathos comes in with the Latinate pun on 'aspire'.

> Th' insulted sea with humbler thoughts he gains,
> A single skiff to speed his flight remains;
> Th' incumber'd oar scarce leaves the dreaded coast
> Through purple billows and a floating host.

However many men have bled into the sea, we know that they never made it look purple; and yet we know that a single drop of blood must purple the sea to some tiny extent. Again, however many men fall dead into the sea, we know that they can never look like a floating host, although we know that that is what they are. Johnson, going behind the sense-impression to what he deduces from it, produces an effect which is farcical, grotesque and horrific all at once. It seems to me comparable with what Mr. Wilson Knight calls the 'tragedy of the grotesque' in *King Lear* ('Horns whelked and waved like the enridged sea'), or what Mr. Eliot found in Marlowe's *Jew of Malta* and *Dido Queen of Carthage*:

> At last, the soldiers pull'd her by the heels,
> And swung her howling in the empty air . . . .

Mr. Eliot calls this "intense and serious and indubitably great poetry, which, like some great painting and sculpture, attains its effects by something not unlike caricature". Johnson's lines, though they use a different method, seem to me to answer to the same description. They enliven a metaphor gone dead.

In the same way, though to different effect, Goldsmith enlivens the metaphor gone dead in the locution 'smiling land':

> As some fair female, unadorn'd and plain,
> Secure to please while youth confirms her reign,
> Slights every borrow'd charm that dress supplies,
> Nor shares with art the triumph of her eyes;

But when those charms are pass'd, for charms are frail,
When time advances, and when lovers fail,
She then shines forth, solicitous to bless,
In all the glaring impotence of dress:
Thus fares the land, by luxury betray'd,
In nature's simplest charms at first array'd:
But verging to decline, its splendours rise,
Its vistas strike, its palaces surprise;
While, scourged by famine, from the smiling land
The mournful peasant leads his humble band;
And while he sinks, without one arm to save,
The country blooms—a garden and a grave.

I do not pretend to explain the triumphant felicity of 'the glaring impotence of dress'. But one cannot miss the startling force given to 'smiling land', when it is seen to smile with heartless indifference on the ruined peasant. The smiling is far more powerful than the more specific 'blooms'. And it is more powerful because we know that in Goldsmith's verse it would have smiled though no peasant had been ruined; whereas Thomas Hardy would not have made it smile unless there were the peasant to be smiled on.

In this passage Goldsmith renovates, too, his conventional verbs. All vistas are striking; but Goldsmith's vistas strike like impotence, and like a plague. As we noted earlier, in this verse the vehicle of metaphor is often the verb. And verbs, like the other parts of speech, are often generalized:

> Here where no springs in murmurs break away,
> Or moss-crowned fountains mitigate the day.

Collins' verb is entirely abstract. It does the verb's proper work, describing not appearance but function, and, by implication, function in a divine scheme. Verbs, like epithets, can be made deliberately at odds with the appearance of the actions they denote:

> Who dash'd the plum-trees from the blossomy ridge?
> From bank to bank who threw the baby bridge . . .?[1]

The vandal and the jerry-builder do not work so fast. In our day the image of the hairy arm, in one hard movement upsetting an orchard, is almost true to reality. Yet even those who have seen a bulldozer at work must admit that the word 'dashed' is something of an exaggeration. In Ebenezer Elliott's day, this word, like 'threw', belied more blatantly the evidence of the senses. Yet Elliott had his authorities, and could appeal to literary precedent for the one usage, and to the language of architects and engineers for the other. Moreover, the word 'dashed', although it belies the appearance, corresponds to the truth of vandalism. Still more to the purpose is 'threw', which has the same connotations of rude violence. It is, as we have said, prosaic or conversational, and, after the literary 'dash'd', it roots the language in sober reality. Finally it has, in conjunction with 'baby bridge', a valuable effect of scornful comedy, as if the gimcrack toy in the villa's garden could indeed be tossed into place by the improver's arm.

At its most powerful this sort of usage can express by metaphor a whole view of human life and destiny. This happens in Cowper's "Castaway":

[1] This example is from "The Splendid Village". Elliott, alas, is still embalmed in the histories as "The Corn-law Rhymer". But the loose couplets in his early work are far superior to what appears in the anthologies.

> At length, his transient respite past,
>   His comrades, who before
> Had heard his voice in every blast,
>   Could catch the sound no more:
> For then, by toil subdued, he drank
> The stifling wave, and then he sank.

'Stifling' is a characteristic use of the participial adjective. It generalizes the fact of drowning, because 'stifling' is equally applicable to all the ways of dying; and so it affects us as dry, chastening and logical. More powerful still, in the same way, is 'drank'. For drinking we think of as a wilful imbibing for pleasure, whereas Cowper generalizes it to mean all drawings in of liquid to the throat. This is horrible, and strikes to the heart of Cowper's view of human life. For Cowper the Calvinist maintained that, even in a world of rigid predestination, the salvation or damnation of the soul was still the responsibility of the individual. He had cried out, in "Truth",

> Charge not, with light sufficient and left free,
> Your wilful suicide on God's decree.

By presenting the rush of water into the drowning throat as a voluntary act of 'drinking', Cowper brings this idea to appalling life. The death of the castaway is 'wilful suicide'. And the one word 'drank', in this place, takes up all the Calvinist arguments of free-will and fate. The generalizing word re-creates the metaphor.

(v) *Circumlocution*

The generalizing habit, the habit of personifying, and the habit of talking round—these are the features we are often asked to see as the vices of much eighteenth-century writing in verse. I have tried to show that personifications and generalizations are often the sources of the most poetic effects in this writing, and also that they are often the way in which the poet purifies the spoken language. The same is true, I believe, of the habit of talking round.

In this verse talking round takes two distinct forms, a distinction which we roughly retain when we speak of periphrasis in some cases, and circumlocution in others. Periphrastic writing can be dealt with fairly shortly, on the lines of an argument broached already. We can take, for a ludicrous instance, the schoolroom example, 'denizen of the deep', as a periphrasis for 'fish'. Needless to say, if we hunted up a case in which this periphrasis was used, we should probably find the use made of it was ludicrous and vicious. For the moment I am concerned only to show how it need not be vicious, by supposing a case in which it was used with effect. It was observed that conventional epithets were sometimes justifiable, as classificatory rather than specific or particular. In the same way it is not hard to think of a case in which the poet, ranging over the natural creation, to draw out of it the divine scheme of plenitude, should wish to present fish as creatures of the sea, birds as creatures of air, beasts as creatures of earth. If the poet's intention was not to see fish in and for themselves, but as one class of the natural hierarchy, it would be proper for him to present them as 'denizens of the deep'. If he added 'finny'—'finny denizens'—he might still be right, if he wanted to present the scheme in some minuteness and distinguish sea-creatures with fins from those without fins.

54

Of course this is special pleading. But we can see how the principle could be applied in practice, if we consider three typical periphrases:

> A Tyger roaming for his prey,
> Sprung on a Trav'ler in the way;
> The prostrate game a Lion spies,
> And on the greedy tyrant flies:
> With mingled roar resounds the wood,
> Their teeth, their claws distil with blood;
> Till vanquish'd by the Lion's strength,
> The spotted foe extends his length.
> The man besought the shaggy lord,
> And on his knees for life implor'd.

'The prostrate game' is correct and dryly pleasant; for we look on the man through the eyes of the lion, and this is how he appears to the beast. But Gay writes here as a fabulist, that is, as a moralist peculiarly interested in the animal creation as a hierarchy of signs acknowledging the creative wisdom. And from this point of view, as the lion is king of beasts, it is correct and exact to denote him by 'the shaggy lord'. But even if a tiger were spotted, it would be trivial and annoying to describe him as 'The spotted foe'. This does not put him in his place in the hierarchy, and although 'foe' defines his relationship to the lion, it is a definition we could have done without. The locution for the tiger is vicious, as the locutions for the man and the lion are not.

Circumlocution is another matter. The trouble with this diction, we hear it said, is its limitation. For all assemblies of trees there is the convenient generality 'grove', for all movements of air the convenient 'gale'. But what is to be done when it is necessary to write of

sofas, cucumbers and billiard-balls? We are led to think
that for the eighteenth-century poet such things were
merely unpoetic, and that he evaded, when possible,
treatment of them. When evasion was impossible (so
the argument runs) he talked round them. Now it is
true to say that these poets talked round these things;
but it is not true that they evaded them. On the contrary, some of the poets welcomed them. When Cowper began, 'I sing the sofa', he wrote "The Task", a
serious discursive poem, not a comical *tour de force*.
The task that he set himself was not arbitrary or fanci-
ful; in a sense it was the task of all his sort of poetry,
the task of seeing the minutiae of social life in the light
of moral truths. And the poem really is about sofas. It
does not depart from the sofa, never to return. It circles
back on the sofa time and again, and on kindred objects
like reading-lamps and cards and newspapers. The
theme is always the sofa, for the theme is the justification of secluded domestic life, that life of which the
sofa is the emblem.

In fact, the whole poem is one vast circumlocution,
and it is built out of repeated circumlocutions on a
smaller scale. Here for instance, Cowper talks round the
cucumber:

> To raise the prickly and green-coated gourd
> So grateful to the palate, and when rare
> So coveted, else base and disesteemed,—
> Food for the vulgar merely,—is an art
> That toiling ages have but just matured,
> And at this moment unessayed in song.
> Yet gnats have had, and frogs and mice long since
> Their eulogy; those sang the Mantuan bard,
> And these the Grecian in ennobling strains;

And in thy numbers, Phillips, shines for aye
The solitary shilling. Pardon then,
Ye sage dispensers of poetic fame,
The ambition of one meaner far, whose powers
Presuming an attempt not less sublime,
Pant for the praise of dressing to the taste
Of critic appetite, no sordid fare,
A cucumber, while costly yet and scarce.

The circumlocution, we observe, is not adopted to
avoid mentioning a supposedly vulgar object, but to
prepare and apologize for its introduction. The poet
gradually lets down the tone until the cucumber can be
introduced. This gradual introduction makes a case
which will bear scrutiny for seeing the cucumber in
generalized terms, in terms of those selected generali-
ties within which the whole poem is working. Thus
the phrase, 'when rare So coveted, else base and
disesteemed', chooses just that aspect of the fruit which
is relevant to Cowper's theme. He is concerned with
the corruption of fashionable life, the metropolitan
corruption to which this account of his gardening is to
be a contrast.

The tone of course is humorous, but humorous in
a special way. Humour, when allied to circumlocution,
is suspect. It is the vice of the schoolboy's magazine
and of some tiresome writing by Charles Lamb. But
this is the humour of the mock-heroic, not of the
whimsy; it is comical in parts, but serious in sum.
Cowper's humour plays round the ideas of modesty
and ambition. His modesty is serious when he compares his poetic activity with that of gardeners who
work, through generations, to acclimatize a fruit. His

E   57

ambition is serious when he claims to write and to esteem only verse which is morally instructive. His modesty is ironical when he agrees that he can praise the cucumber only while it is scarce. And his ambition is ironical when he thinks to rival Virgil, by recommending the cucumber to the palates of Georgian London. By comparison with this, Wordsworth in "Simon Lee" seems singularly inflexible. Wordsworth sees no reason why swollen ankles should be vulgar or comical, and he is determined to write as if they are not. Cowper may think that the idea of the cucumber as vulgar is part of our unredeemed frivolity; but he does not blink the fact that vulgar and comical they are or seem. By irony and exaggeration, he destroys these false barriers even as he acknowledges them.

This is the place to take up some suggestions I have thrown out already, about diversity of tone in this poetry, and in all poetry which employs chaste diction. It may be agreed that Cowper's circumlocution is better than Wordsworth's bathos. Yet, it may be objected, both poets go wrong in pitching their styles, from the start, in too high a key. If Cowper had not adopted a lofty tone, he would not have needed to let it down to accommodate the cucumber. It may even be felt that the bane of eighteenth-century verse is the lofty tone it seems forced to adopt on all occasions. This may be partly what Mr. Eliot meant when he called the bad verse of the period, 'intolerably poetical'. Where the good poets are concerned, one retorts in one way by pointing to "John Gilpin" or Goldsmith's "Haunch of Venison", poems where the tone is not lofty. It may be replied that these, pleasant though they are, are trivial at best. But surely that is the point; these poets took a serious view of their profession, and where the business in hand was of such moment as instruction in moral conduct, they can hardly be blamed for being lofty about it. Even Puttenham allowed that, while the speech of peasants would usually demand the base style, yet, when they treated of weighty matters of 'civil regiment', the style should be lofty. It could be said, of Johnson, Goldsmith and Cowper, that their concern in their serious verse was always 'civil regiment'. Certainly this is the theme of "The Task"; and Cowper was right, therefore, to maintain an elevated tone.

It may be thought, incidentally, that by admitting Cowper's predilection for the lofty tone, I come near to denying that I find in him that tie with conversational usage which I have put forward as one of the two conditions of chastity in diction. But this is not so. For Puttenham, the three styles of verse (the lofty, the mean, the base) are equally closely in touch with spoken usage. The lofty style uses the speech of the court; the mean style, the speech of merchants and yeomanry; the base style, the speech of menial trades and the peasantry. However much the social structure may have changed since Puttenham's day, there is no excuse for supposing (as we often do) that the loftier the verse, the less conversational. An example of modern verse, at once lofty and conversational, I take to be Yeats' "Lament for Robert Gregory".[1]

Circumlocution is vicious when it is merely prolix.

[1] The point is neatly made by C. S. Lewis, describing the lofty and chaste diction of Gower (*Allegory of Love*, p. 201).

Cowper's procedure can be as inflexible as Wordsworth's:

> Nor envies he aught more their idle sport
> Who pant with application misapplied
> To trivial toys, and pushing ivory balls
> Across the velvet level, feel a joy
> Akin to rapture, when the bauble finds
> Its destined goal of difficult access.

We can echo Mr. Eliot and say of this that what the
poet has to say appears surprised at the way in which
he chooses to say it. The tone is not humorous at all;
compare, for instance, the different force of 'pant' in
this passage and in the lines on the cucumber. The
substance of what the poet has to say is said already in
the one phrase 'misapplied to . . . toys'. The rest is
verbose, repeating that idea in less powerful ways.
This passage comes from Book VI of "The Task",
where Cowper, preparing for a peroration, becomes
more and more Miltonic. Cowper's blank verse is not
substantially Miltonic.[1] But it is true that when he
approaches the mock-heroic effect, Cowper draws upon
Milton, where Johnson draws upon Dryden. At such
moments Cowper uses the Miltonic magniloquence
for his own purposes, and with success. Undoubtedly,
though, some of Cowper's blank verse is Miltonic in
the bad sense that it challenges comparison with Milton
and is damned by the comparison. In view of Cowper's

---

[1] Cf. Cowper in a letter (quoted by Gilbert Thomas, *William
Cowper and the Eighteenth Century*, p. 217): "Milton's manner was
peculiar. So is Thomson's. He that should write like either of them,
would, in my judgment, deserve the name of a copyist, but not of a
poet. A judicious and sensible reader therefore . . . will not say that
my manner is not good, because it does not resemble theirs, but will
rather consider what it is in itself."

repudiation of the Miltonic model, it is fair to suppose that where the magniloquence asserts itself to no mock-heroic effect, it is a sign of flagging invention. And this is surely what happens here. 'Its destined goal of difficult access' has 'a Miltonic grandeur'. In other words its grandeur is merely verbal and sonorous, reaping the easy reward of culminating rhythms. That was why, perhaps, the paragraph had to run to length through an agglomeration of subordinate phrases. Nothing in the simple idea justifies this length or this complication. In the 'grandeur' of the last line, 'destined' only repeats the notion of 'application'; and it cheapens shockingly the idea of destiny. Only the billiard-player has destined the ball for a pocket, but in the scheme of the Miltonic grandeur the word trumpets like Jehovah's predestination of Adam. This is adulteration of the spoken tongue.

Thus circumlocution is neither good nor bad in itself. When it is good, it ensures a consistent tone of discourse. And if, as I. A. Richards maintained, tone is an aspect of meaning, then to preserve a consistent tone is one way of defining meanings and purifying the language. After all, what is "The Castaway" but a circumlocutory account of Cowper's damnation?

IV

POETIC DICTION AND PROSAIC
STRENGTH

A PURE poetic diction can purify the national language by enlivening metaphors gone dead. But
since nearly all meanings are metaphorical by origin,
we have to say that poetry re-creates a metaphor when-
ever it makes us aware, with new or renewed nicety, of
the meaning of almost any word. To say this is to use
'metaphor' in a specially extended sense. And in general
there is something ludicrous about the way modern
criticism circles round and round 'metaphor', explaining
poetry more and more in terms of 'images'; this is
sufficient reason for not extending the use of the word
even further, and if 'metaphor' is taken in a more usual
and restricted sense, one of the conclusions to be derived
from the present study is that poetry can be written in
unmetaphorical language. This is no new discovery—
we have seen it affirmed, in different ways, by both
Goldsmith and Wordsworth—but it is an aspect of
poetry little considered to-day. In the Prologue to "A
Word to the Wise", Johnson renovates the word
'Bounty', and makes us more conscious of its meaning.
In a sense he does so by re-creating a metaphor
gone dead in the word, but to say so is to use 'metaphor' in a specially extended sense; and it is better,
when dealing with this sort of achievement, to forget
about metaphor and, following Johnson, to call it
'strength'.

Johnson used 'strength', and defined it, sufficiently for his purpose, in the *Life of Denham*:

> The strength of Denham, which Pope so emphatically mentions, is to be found in many lines and couplets, which convey much meaning in few words, and exhibit the sentiment with more weight than bulk.

The term 'strength' was much used by critics in the seventeenth century, and Johnson agrees, in substance though not in sentiment, with Hobbes:

> To this palpable darkness I may also add the ambitious obscurity of expressing more than is perfectly conceived, or perfect conception in fewer words than it requires, which expressions, though they have had the honour to be called strong lines, are indeed no better than riddles. . . .[1]

By Hobbes' time 'strength' was identified with Clevelandism, that is, with a decadent and frivolous form of 'conceited' and hyperbolical writing; and this explains Hobbes' dislike of compression and concentration, when pursued as ends in themselves, under pressure of no informing purpose or feeling. Throughout the seventeenth century 'strong' or 'masculine' writing is associated with what modern critics have called 'the line of Wit', and others, the 'marinist' or 'metaphysical' strain. But Pope and Johnson were right, I think, when they judged that Denham had saved the essential 'strength', the concentration, while disengaging it from the hyperbolical conceit.

This view is confirmed by the three examples from Denham which Johnson considered. Because Denham

[1] Hobbes, essay on "Gondibert" (1651). See Appendix B for a sketch of the history of 'strength' as a term of criticism in the seventeenth century.

is unjustly neglected to-day, I make no excuse for quoting these pieces again.[1] The first is a passage on the Thames, from "Cooper's Hill":

> Though with those streams he no resemblance hold,
> Whose foam is amber, and their gravel gold;
> His genuine and less guilty wealth t'explore,
> Search not his bottom, but survey his shore.

This is still a conceit, though muted and less hyperbolical than those we remember from Marvell or Donne. Its distinction cannot be better phrased than by Johnson—it exhibits the sentiment with more weight than bulk. The same is true of Johnson's second example, the lines on Strafford:

> His wisdom such, at once it did appear
> Three Kingdoms' wonder, and three Kingdoms' fear;
> While single he stood forth, and seem'd, although
> Each had an army, as an equal foe.
> Such was his force of eloquence, to make
> The hearers more concern'd than he that spake;
> Each seem'd to act that part he came to see,
> And none was more a looker-on than he;
> So did he move our passions, some were known
> To wish, for the defence, the crime their own.
> Now private pity strove with publick hate,
> Reason with rage, and eloquence with fate.

The hyperbole here is as delightfully arrogant as the hyperboles of Marvell; but it is achieved not at all in Marvell's way. The ghost of a 'conceited' image hovers over the third and fourth lines, but thereafter the hyperbole, and the concentration which goes with it, is

[1] For the literary historians, Denham and Waller make up one set of twins, as Shenstone and Akenside sometimes make up another. The coupling is unjust to Denham, as it is to Shenstone.

carried through in conversational and unmetaphorical language, chiefly by apt handling of syntax. And the reader has to define anew each of the words clustered and opposed in the last couplet, 'private' and 'public', 'reason' and 'rage', 'eloquence' and 'fate'. Each word, arranged thus artfully with and against the others, and taking up the exposition which went before, takes on new life, defined freshly and closely. This is to purify the language. It occurs more clearly still in a passage on Cowley:

> To him no author was unknown,
> Yet what he wrote was all his own;
> Horace's wit and Virgil's state,
> He did not steal, but emulate!
> And when he would like them appear,
> Their garb, but not their cloaths, did wear.

It had not occurred to the reader that the distinction between 'garb' and 'clothes' was so fine yet so definite. It is forced on his attention in a way that is salutary, pleasing, and relevant to the poet's theme.

Of another excerpt, Johnson says:

so much meaning is comprised in so few words; the particulars of resemblance are so perspicaciously collected, and every mode of excellence separated from its adjacent fault by so nice a line of limitation; the different parts of the sentence are so accurately adjusted; and the flow of the last couplet is so smooth and sweet; that the passage, however celebrated, has not been praised above its merit.

I know no better account of the effect of prosaic 'strength' and pure diction in poetry. These are Johnson's comments on "The four verses, which, since

Dryden has commended them, almost every writer for a century past has imitated".[1] They appear in "Cooper's Hill":

> O could I flow like thee, and make thy stream
> My great example, as it is my theme!
> Though deep, yet clear, though gentle, yet not dull;
> Strong without rage, without o'erflowing full.

This is what it describes, a prosaic strength, concentrated and discriminating, which purifies the language as it uses it. It possesses a distinction which has nothing to do with metaphor; and Johnson indeed affirms that it would be better without those metaphors it has:

> The lines are in themselves not perfect; for most of the words, thus artfully opposed, are to be understood simply on one side of the comparison, and metaphorically on the other; and if there be any language which does not express intellectual operations by material images, into that language they cannot be translated.

Is a poem the better the more it is translatable? We may wonder.[2] But in any case Johnson's objection emphasizes that this sort of achievement is the greater according as the language is less figurative.

It seems to me that this distinction has just reappeared in English poetry, after too long an absence:

---

[1] And the poets continued to imitate; cf. Cowper's wretched attempt, in "Conversation":

> "A veteran warrior in the Christian field,
> Who never saw the sword he could not wield;
> Grave without dullness, learned without pride,
> Exact, yet not precise, though meek, keen-eyed."

[2] T. S. Eliot comes near to saying that translatability is a test of one sort of poetic excellence. According to him, it is a sign of the excellence of some of Dante.

> If I think, again, of this place,
> And of people, not wholly commendable,
> Of no immediate kin or kindness,
> But some of peculiar genius,
> All touched by a common genius,
> United in the strife which divided them. . . .

If I want to find the ancestry, in English verse, of this
nicety of statement, I have to go, if not with Johnson
to Denham, then to Ben Jonson or Greville or Dryden:

> . . . To like what you lik'd, and at Masques or Playes
> Commend the self-same Actors, the same wayes;
> Ask how you did? and often with intent
> Of being officious, grow impertinent. . . .[1]

> Is it the mark or majesty of Power
> To make offences that it may forgive?[2]

> Reveal'd Religion first informed thy sight,
> And Reason saw not till Faith sprung the Light.
> Hence all thy Natural Worship takes the source:
> 'Tis Revelation what thou think'st Discourse.[3]

Or I can find it in Johnson and in Thomas Parnell.[4]
In other poets, it occurs only with a difference. In
Shakespeare the prosaic statement is only a momentary
shaft of light through the foliage of metaphor. In Pope
it is superbly clear and taut, but always pointed, limited
in tone. In Wordsworth what seems to be statement

---

[1] 'Officious' (in its Latinate sense, as in Johnson's "Elegy on Robert
Levett") defines and is defined by 'impertinent'. The passage is from
Jonson, "Underwoods", xxxix.

[2] The question is rhetorical and has the effect of nice and momentous
statement.

[3] 'Discourse' is re-defined by striking off from 'Revelation'.

[4] See Appendix A for an appreciation of the diction of Parnell.

is really rumination.[1] Where this strength occurs in poetry, that poetry must be said to have the virtues of good prose.

This strength of statement is found most often in a chaste or pure diction, because it goes together with economy in metaphor; and such economy is a feature of such a diction. It is achieved by judgment and taste, and it preserves the tone of the centre, a sort of urbanity. It purifies the spoken tongue, for it makes the reader alive to nice meanings. The poet who tries for such chastity and strength will never have his reader's love, but he may have his esteem. As C. S. Lewis says of John Gower:

> He can be dull: he can never be affected, strident, or ridiculous.

And as T. S. Eliot says of a greater master:

> The language of each great English poet is his own language; the language of Dante is the perfection of a common language. In a sense, it is more pedestrian than that of Dryden or Pope. If you follow Dante without talent, you will at worst be pedestrian and flat; if you follow Shakespeare or Pope without talent, you will make an utter fool of yourself.

It seems to follow that if we want to find in English 'the perfection of a common language' (and that is a good definition of pure diction) we should look not among our great poets, but among our good ones. Gower and Greville and Denham, Parnell and Goldsmith, Johnson and Cowper, seem to me good poets of this sort.

Mr. Eliot has proved as good as his word. In the "Four Quartets" his verse has the virtues of good prose:

[1] Cf. F. R. Leavis, *Revaluation*, p. 162.

POETIC DICTION AND PROSAIC STRENGTH

                         And every phrase
And sentence that is right (where every word is at home,
Taking its place to support the others,
The word neither diffident nor ostentatious,
An easy commerce of the old and the new,
The common word exact without vulgarity,
The formal word precise but not pedantic,
The complete consort dancing together)
Every phrase and every sentence is an end and a beginning,
Every poem an epitaph.

Of these lines we must say, as of Denham's lines, that
they are what they describe. These should engage the
twentieth century as those did the eighteenth.

V

THE CLASSICISM OF CHARLES WESLEY

IN so-called lyrical poetry we may expect to find less of those felicities which I have here connected with the idea of a chaste diction. Certainly this will be so, so long as we consider 'lyrical' and 'didactic' poetry as poles apart. They are often so considered, and therefore many readers will applaud the late-Augustan poets as masters of didactic verse, for what that is worth (and the usual implication is that it is worth very little), at the same time as they regret the scarcity in the period of notable lyrical verse. On the other hand, though in much the same way, I have heard it asserted that the eighteenth century is poor in religious poetry, because (so we assume) religious poetry is not didactic either. This attitude is, of course, a legacy from the long period when religious experience was considered almost exclusively a matter of fervent feeling, and dogma was disreputable. The point to be made for the present purpose is that between these two preconceptions, about 'lyrical' poetry on the one hand and 'religious' poetry on the other, a large body of the best verse of this period goes unregarded altogether. I mean the hymns of Cowper and Charles Wesley and John Newton, not to mention the rather earlier achievements of Doddridge and Watts. 'Lyrical' or not, 'religious' or not (and to my mind it is as absurd to deny them the one status as the other), these poems manifest the same virtues as the secular poetry of the period; and to prove that they do so is to show that such qualities as prosaic strength, exactness and urbanity are not to be looked for only in poetry of a special and very limited kind, but can flourish and give pleasure in kinds of poetry which seem very different from "The Vanity of Human Wishes" or even "The Deserted Village".

It must be admitted from the start that there is something reasonable in a reluctance to consider hymns as merely one genre of poetic writing. As Bernard Manning remarks:

A hymn like "Jesu, Lover of my soul" may be poor religious poetry: but, in face of its place in English religion, only imbecility will declare it a poor hymn.[1]

That is a comment from the point of view of the hymnologist. As readers of poetry, our difficulties are, first, the need to disentangle, in the effect made upon us by a hymn, the appeal which is literary from others which derive from our own religious persuasions, our memory of musical melodies, or even such less tangible attractions as childhood associations; and, secondly, I think, our sense of an unfair advantage enjoyed by the hymnwriter over other poets. The themes of the hymn-writer are, to use a favourite late-Augustan expression, so important, that our sense of their urgency can excuse or even conceal in our minds the poverty of their expression. We feel that the hymn-writer, unlike the secular poet, has only to avoid certain fairly obvious pit-falls in order that his message may carry him through. In the poet mere competence is not enough; in the writer of hymns, we feel, it is. And it is probably taken for

[1] Bernard L. Manning, *The Hymns of Wesley and Watts* (Epworth Press), p. 109.

granted, among those who have never exerted themselves to see Wesley's hymns as literature, that his acknowledged pre-eminence is a matter of metrical facility, resourcefulness in rhyme, and a dead level of honest and sober language.

As a matter of fact, this is true of a good deal of Wesley's writing. Inevitably, writing so much, he composed many good hymns which are undistinguished or indifferent poems. But it requires, after all, no great exertion to appreciate other pieces as good poems in their own right. In particular it is not true that his language is all on one level. If it were so, he would be incapable of the poignant simplicity which is one of his best effects; for that effect, as in *King Lear* ('Pray you, undo this button') is brought about by sudden and calculated descent from a relatively elaborate level of language:

> Sinners, believe the gospel word,
>   Jesus is come your souls to save!
> Jesus is come, your common Lord;
>   Pardon ye all through Him may have,
> May now be saved, whoever will;
> This Man receiveth sinners still.[1]

The piercing directness of that last line is an achievement of literary form. As Ezra Pound says:

Neither prose nor drama can attain poetic intensity save by construction, almost by scenario; by so arranging the circumstance that some perfectly simple speech, perception, dogmatic statement appears in abnormal vigour. Thus when Frederic in *L'Education* observes Mme. Arnoux's shoe-laces as she is de-

[1] "The Methodist Hymn-book" (1904), no. 283.

scending the stair; or in Turgenev the quotation of a Russian proverb about the 'heart of another', or 'Nothing but death is irrevocable' towards the end of *Nichée de Gentilshommes*.[1]

The construction of Wesley's hymn is an example of 'scenario' in this sense, and his last line reaps the reward in 'abnormal vigour'. It is one of Wesley's most common devices.[2] His is a sophisticated art.

It is not different in kind from that of his contemporaries, the secular poets. For instance, John Wesley was right when he claimed for his brother's verse that it was 'scriptural', in the sense that almost every metaphor or striking turn of phrase can be traced to a biblical original. But this does not mean that Wesley was restricted and hampered in his composition; still less that he was condemned to a sectarian jargon, like Zeal-of-the-Land Busy. On the contrary, it means that Wesley enjoyed, as Pope did or Johnson, a sort of extra poetic dimension. He could expect his congregations to know Scripture as Johnson and Pope could expect their readers to know Virgil and Horace. All of them therefore had given to them a sort of literary resource which Mr. Eliot, for instance, has had to re-create for himself. Johnson could refer to Horace, and Wesley to Isaiah, subtly and discreetly; whereas Mr. Eliot when he wants to refer to Dante, Baudelaire or Webster, has, in "The Waste Land", to quote at length and draw the reader's attention in a note. A critic has well described this Augustan myth as 'a field of force' lying behind the most apparently guileless of eighteenth-century poems; Wesley's poetry

[1] Ezra Pound, *Make it New*, p. 289.
[2] Cf. "Hymn-book", nos. 192, 594.

can draw upon a field no less powerful. The modern reader will miss all but the most obvious of the Scriptural references, just as he will miss all but the loudest classical echoes in Pope. A crude example is no. 256 in the "Hymn-book":

> Expand Thy wings, celestial Dove,
>> Brood o'er our nature's night;
> On our disordered spirits move,
>> And let there now be light.

The activity of the Holy Spirit in the human soul is described in terms which recall the Creative Spirit in Genesis; and as a result the word 'disordered' is set against the vast image of primeval chaos. It is the exact word; but by its very exactness, like the epithets of Johnson, it gives a dry effect of under-statement, which creates the urbane tone.

Occasionally, Wesley refers to other than revealed writings. Bernard Manning gives an example:[1]

> Lord, we Thy will obey,
>> And in Thy pleasure rest;
> We, only we, can say,
>> "Whatever is, is best."
> Faith, mighty faith, the promise sees,
>> And looks to that alone;
> Laughs at impossibilities,
>> And cries, "It shall be done!"

The reference, in line 4, is to Pope's "Whatever is, is right". Similar are the lines in "Christ the Lord is risen to-day":

[1] Manning, *op. cit.* pp. 73, 74.

74

> Lives again our glorious King!
> Where, O death, is now thy sting?
> Once He died our souls to save:
> Where's thy victory, boasting grave?[1]

Or, again, any number of references to 'the undistinguished grave' come to life with the twist:

> Love, like death, hath all destroyed,
> Rendered all distinctions void;

This habit of inconspicuous reference to previous literature and especially to a hallowed canon, classical or scriptural, is obviously related to what I have argued is the distinguishing excellence of a pure diction, the practice of refurbishing old metaphors gone dead, rather than the hunting out of new ones. Because Wesley aimed to be scriptural, he coined even fewer novel metaphors than his secular contemporaries did. When he does take the liberty, he is capable, as Cowper is,[2] of a seventeenth-century wit:

> Love's redeeming work is done;
> Fought the fight, the battle won;
> Lo! the sun's eclipse is o'er;
> Lo! he sets in blood no more.[3]

And sometimes the whole conceit is carried in one word:

---

[1] The same famous Popian tag is treated in the same way in no. 474:
> "O death! where is thy sting? Where now
> Thy boasted victory, O grave?
> Who shall contend with God? or who
> Can hurt whom God delights to save?"

[2] Cf. the gypsies in "The Task":
> "The sportive wind blows wide
> Their fluttering rags, and shows a tawny skin,
> The vellum of the pedigree they claim."

[3] "Hymn-book", no. 170.

> Captain of our salvation, take
>> The souls we here present to Thee,
> And fit for Thy great service make
>> These heirs of immortality;
> And let them in Thine image rise,
> And then transplant to paradise.[1]

But more typically he takes a dead metaphor and en-livens it:

> Strike with the hammer of Thy word,
>> And break these hearts of stone.[2]

Or again:

> Impoverish, Lord, and then relieve
>> And then enrich the poor;
> The knowledge of our sickness give,
>> The knowledge of our cure.
>
> That blessed sense of guilt impart,
>> And then remove the load;
> Trouble, and wash the troubled heart
>> In the atoning blood.[3]

And this is only the simplest version of this rejuvena-tion. As with the secular poets, so with Wesley, the enlivening of dead metaphors is in the end indistinguish-able from all those arrangements of words which, by contrast, antithesis, juxtaposition, force us to re-define meanings and pick our words with nicety:

> His adorable will
> Let us gladly fulfil,
> And our talents improve,
> By the patience of hope and the labour of love.[4]

[1] "Hymn-book", no. 894.   [2] *Ibid.* no. 305.
[3] *Ibid.*   [4] *Ibid.* no. 930.

Whatever the effect of this on the congregations of Wesley's time, for us both 'adorable' and 'labour of love' are shockingly cheapened expressions which, once we have read Wesley's verse, become once again taut and definite. In Wesley, as in Johnson, the blunted meaning or the buried metaphor comes sharp and live again in a sort of Latinate pun:

> This instant now I may receive
>> The answer of His powerful prayer;
> This instant now by Him I live,
>> His prevalence with God declare;[1]

And sometimes too, as in the Prologue to "A Word to the Wise", pairs of abstractions are generalized in parallel, with an effect of mounting tension:

> The atonement of thy blood apply,
>> Till faith to sight improve,
> Till hope in full fruition die,
>> And all my soul be love.[2]

—where 'faith' opposed to 'sight', is generalized to 'hope', as 'sight' is to 'love'.

The use of language is always responsible. There is a Johnsonian weighing of epithets—'as pure, as even and as strong', 'obscurely safe', 'spotless and peaceable and kind'. A word such as 'seer' (in no. 196 of the "Hymn-book") is not employed for its affecting connotations, but exactly, with the etymologist's exactness; and in the same hymn, for instance, as much can be said of 'signify', 'cancelled', 'meritorious', each offering a different temptation to looseness yet always used strictly for the sense.

[1] "Hymn-book", no. 192.   [2] *Ibid.* no. 532.

77

It is only from this point of view that one sees the true force of Wesley's Latinisms. They are not threaded on the staple Anglo-Saxon of his diction in order merely to give a pleasing variety in sound and pace (though they do that incidentally) but so that Saxon and classical elements can criss-cross and light up each the other's meaning. Occasionally there occur bad pseudo-Miltonic Latinisms ('Implunged in the crystal abyss', '. . . through life's disparted wave . . .') but in general the Latinisms are Johnsonian:

> Author of faith appear!
> Be Thou its finisher;[1]

—where the ungainly 'finisher' is there to remind us that 'Author' means 'originator'. And the ungainliness disappears when the same word-play is handled again:

> Author of faith, eternal Word,
>> Whose Spirit breathes the active flame;
> Faith, like its Finisher and Lord,
>> To-day, as yesterday the same.[2]

Sometimes the Anglo-Saxon word, when it comes, seems to take us by the throat:

> The millennial year
> Rushes on to our view, and eternity's here.[3]

At its best, the Latinism can be, in Bernard Manning's phrase, the 'classic summary' of a whole doctrine:

> Adam, descended from above!
> Federal Head of all mankind.

And in the process it purifies the language of the tribe.

[1] "Hymn-book", no. 630. [2] *Ibid.* no. 345. [3] *Ibid.* no. 930.

As the same critic remarks of another such, "congregations bred on such stuff should not suffer from flabbiness of thought".[1]

It is obvious that Wesley's verse exhibits these virtues because it is throughout doctrinal, that is, didactic. His hymns are not, like most later hymns, so many geysers of warm 'feeling'. And yet, heaven knows, the 'feeling' is there. We respect its integrity and we take its force just because it is not offered in isolation but together with its occasion, an occasion grasped and presented with keen and sinewy intelligence. Intelligence comes into the poetry of this period not as contraband, smuggled into a conceit as 'ingenuity', or intangibly as ironical tone, but straightforward and didactic. And the intellectual strength does not desiccate the emotions but gives to them validity and force.

Wesley's themes, then, are the central paradoxes of the Christian faith. His favourite figure is oxymoron:

Impassive, He suffers; immortal, He dies.

This is the figure in which Wesley employs his Latinate puns, his 'curial' language, with most force. And sometimes, out of an original oxymoron, flowers a whole growth of crucial paradox:

Victim divine, Thy grace we claim,
    While thus Thy precious death we show:
Once offered up, a spotless Lamb,
    In Thy great temple here below,
Thou didst for all mankind atone,
And standest now before the throne.

[1] Manning, *op. cit.* p. 107.

> Thou standest in the holy place,
> As now for guilty sinners slain:
> The blood of sprinkling speaks, and prays,
> All prevalent for helpless man;
> Thy blood is still our ransom found,
> And speaks salvation all around.
>
> We need not now go up to heaven,
> To bring the long-sought Saviour down;
> Thou art to all already given,
> Thou dost even now Thy banquet crown:
> To every faithful soul appear,
> And show Thy real presence here.[1]

Because the original paradox ('Victim divine') is developed, we realize that it is not an accidental fuzziness like Tennyson's 'divine despair'. Because Christ was both sacrifice and priest, and because the smoke of that atonement both cast a veil and rent it too, we are made conscious that 'invisible' means 'unshowable', what cannot be shown and yet was shown. A common word takes on unusual clarity and force:

In the Methodist chapel, as in the drawing-room, the poet used the language spoken by his hearers. He did not try to heighten, to disrupt, or even, in the first place, to enrich that language, but to sharpen it, to make it more exact and pure, and thereby (paradoxically) more flexible. He seldom used shock-tactics. His concern was not to create a distinctive style, but to contribute to a common stock, to safeguard a heritage and to keep it as bright as new. Ezra Pound remarks:

Anatole France is said to have spent a great deal of time searching for the *least possible* variant that would turn the most

1 "Hymn-book", no. 727.

worn-out and commonest phrases of journalism into something distinguished.

Such research is sometimes termed 'classicism'.

This is the greatest possible remove from the usual English stylist's trend or urge towards a style different from everyone else's.[1]

From this point of view, Charles Wesley is a classical poet, as Dr. Johnson is.

[1] *A B C of Reading*, p. 54.

VI

THE "VANITY OF HUMAN WISHES"
AND "DE VULGARI ELOQUENTIA"

THE connection proposed in the title of this essay is, at first sight, a queer one. The association of Johnson's respectable poem with Dante's treatise on poetic diction must seem bizarre and more than a little gauche. In recent years, Johnson's poem has risen greatly in critical esteem and has attracted the more or less admiring attention of Ezra Pound, T. S. Eliot and F. R. Leavis, to name no more. But there would be a sort of pathetic insularity about any pretence that it is one of the great achievements of European culture, or that Dr. Johnson as poet can, as a result, stand comparison with a figure such as Dante. And Pound, at any rate, will clearly deny to it anything of the sort.[1]

Nevertheless, for the intelligent English reader, to whom a poem in his own tongue must always be more immediate than a poem however illustrious in another—for such a reader, the connection exists. Mr. Eliot, for instance, can use Johnson's poem and Dante's poetry to much the same end—to the one end of insisting that language is not more poetic the further it is removed from the language of prose. It is because, in their view, the poetry of Milton has lent support to this fallacy, that the three critics cited were at one in their depreciation of Milton as in their appreciation of Johnson. And Johnson himself was of their opinion:

[1] *Guide to Kulchur*, pp. 179-181, 183-184, 193.

Gray thought his language more poetical as it was more remote from common use: finding in Dryden *honey redolent of Spring*, an expression that reaches the utmost limits of our language, Gray drove it a little more beyond apprehension by making *gales* to be *redolent of joy and youth*.

In this comment Johnson, by adopting the twin criteria of literary precedent (Dryden) and 'common use', is on the same ground as Ezra Pound when the latter asserts: "The border-line between 'gee whizz' and Milton's tumified dialect must exist".[1] And Pound goes on to say that "Dante in De Vulgari Eloquio, seems to have thought of a good many particulars of the problem". There is some reason, then, for supposing that in Dante's treatise we find a more comprehensive exposition of certain principles of poetic diction, implicit in Johnson's poetry and criticism, and, when found there, embraced by contemporary critics and practising poets as peculiarly relevant to the writing of poetry to-day. In this essay I propose to establish this relevance, and I am concerned with Johnson's poem only by the way, as exhibiting in English and in a small way the principle which Dante promotes. The principle in question is that of purity in poetic diction, and it appears to have been lost to English poetry and criticism between Dr. Johnson and Mr. Pound. After so long an absence from the English scene, it was not to be re-established in a hurry. And because, even after Mr. Eliot's writing and Mr. Pound's, it is still hardly acknowledged, there is some point in revealing it again in its classical expression by Dante. I am concerned then with the treatise, only as it has interest for the English poet and the

[1] Pound, *Letters*, ed. Paige, p. 349.

reader of English poets, not as it takes its place in the canon of Dante's works or in the history of Italian literature.

From this point of view, of the two books which exist, the most interesting portions are chapters xvi, xvii and xviii of Book I, and chapters ii and iv of Book II.

In his first fifteen chapters Dante has insisted first on the unprecedented nature of the speculation he proposes. He distinguishes between the Vulgar Tongue (the vernacular) and 'Grammar', that is, Latin; and decides that the first is 'the nobler as being natural to us'. Speech, he points out, is a specifically human endowment, for angels know each other immediately and have no need of speech; human communication, therefore, is neither instinctive, like that of the brutes, nor spiritual, as with angels, but partakes of both qualities, being 'rational and sensible'. That is, it appeals to the reason but also to the senses.

After so much by way of introduction, Dante devotes four chapters to telling of the first universal language and how it was broken up as a penalty for human presumption in attempting the tower of Babel. The field narrows to Europe, wherein, Dante states, there were once three languages, the Northern or Teutonic, the Greek or Eurasian, and the language then common to 'Spaniards' (i.e. the men of Provence), Frenchmen and Italians. Each of these is now divided further, the last of them into the language of 'oc' (Provençal), the language of 'oil' (French) and the language of 'si' (Italian). After giving examples of the essential identity of French, Provençal and Italian, Dante explains that it is human instability which has produced this progress-

84

ive disintegration, and that it continues to have this effect, setting up provincial dialects inside the languages; hence the need for the artificial stability of Latin. After a digression on the peculiar virtues of French (best, says Dante, for prose), of Provençal (as having the longest established poetic tradition) and of Italian (as the tongue of Cino da Pistoia and Dante himself), the critic surveys the dialects of Italy, and the claims of each of these to be the most 'illustrious'.

All of this seems sufficiently remote from anything of interest to the modern reader. It ceases to be so when Dante remarks that no one of the dialects can be considered the most illustrious, since the best poets have always departed from their own dialect for the purposes of their poetry. This leads him in chapter xvi to the conclusion:

Having, then, found what we were looking for, we declare that the Illustrious, Cardinal, Courtly, and Curial Vulgar Tongue in Italy is that which belongs to all the towns in Italy, but does not appear to belong to any one of them; and is that by which all the local dialects of the Italians are measured, weighed, and compared.[1]

That is, Dante esteems, as T. S. Eliot does, a poetic diction which is not personal and distinctive but 'the perfection of a common language'. From George Puttenham we learn that in Elizabeth's England, as in Dante's Italy, the poet, in forming his diction, had still to consider different sorts of English spoken in different parts of the country. The modern English poet has to

[1] *De Vulgari Eloquentia* (translated A. G. Ferrers Howell, 1890), p. 38.

con over dialects in just the same way, but the dialects are no longer regional ones. Instead there are class-dialects, period-dialects, the jargons of schools, cliques, 'generations', political or religious parties; and the pure diction of the modern poet, like the 'illustrious tongue' of Dante, will be intelligible to all of these elements, but peculiar to none of them.

In chapter xvii Dante explains what he means by calling this language 'illustrious'. That is illustrious 'which shines forth illuminating and illuminated'; and this lustre belongs to things which are exalted either by authority or by training and discipline, and which reflect this lustre on those who follow and honour them. Dante says of the common language of Italian poetry:

> Now, it appears to have been exalted by training, inasmuch as we see it (purified) from so many rude Italian words, involved constructions, faulty expressions, and rustic accents, and brought to such a degree of excellence, clearness, completeness, and polish, as is displayed by Cino of Pistoja and his friend in their *Canzoni*.[1]

This corresponds to what we have said of a pure diction as 'choice', and this choiceness appears, we have said (and Dante implies as much), as "a sense as of words and expressions thrusting at the poem and being fended off from it".

In the next chapter, which is of crucial importance, Dante explains his other three epithets. First, why does he call the poetic language 'cardinal'?

because, as the whole door follows its hinge, and whither the hinge turns the door also turns, whether it be moved inwards or

---

[1] *De Vulgari Eloquentia*, pp. 39, 40.

outwards; so the whole herd of local dialects turns and returns, moves and pauses, according as this (Illustrious language does), which really seems to be the father of a family. Does it not daily root out the thorny bushes from the Italian wood? Does it not daily insert cuttings or plant young trees? What else have its foresters to do but to bring in and take away as has been said? Wherefore it surely deserves to be adorned with so great a name as this.[1]

Herein is implied all that Mr. Eliot has said about the poet's duty 'to purify the language of the tribe', and it supports us in our argument that this purification can only come about through purity, or chastity of diction.

Then, what does Dante mean by 'courtly'?

if we Italians had a Court it would be an Imperial one; and if a Court is a common home of all the realm, and an august ruler of all parts of the realm, it would be fitting that whatever is of such a character as to be common to all (parts) without being peculiar to any should frequent this Court and dwell there; nor is there any other abode worthy of so great an inmate. Such, in fact, seems to be that Vulgar Tongue of which we are speaking; and hence it is that those who frequent all the royal palaces always speak the Illustrious Vulgar Tongue. Hence, also, it happens that our Illustrious Language wanders about like a wayfarer and is welcomed in humble shelters, seeing we have no Court.[2]

This may serve as our justification in linking with the idea of a pure diction all the Arnoldian doctrine, as to Attic prose, that it embodies 'the tone and spirit of the centre', as opposed to the provincial. Dante's 'courtliness' is our 'urbanity'. And from the last sentence quoted we see that for Dante too the question was of a

[1] *De Vulgari Eloquentia*, pp. 40, 41.   [2] *Ibid*. p. 41.

spiritual quality, 'urbanity' as opposed to 'provincial-ism', not of any actual metropolis or any actual provinces, in the sense of the geographer.

Finally, why is the pure diction 'curial'?

because Curiality is nothing else but the justly balanced rule of things which have to be done; and, because the scales required for this kind of balancing are only wont to be found in the most excellent Courts of Justice, it follows that whatever is well balanced in our actions is called Curial. Wherefore, since this Illustrious language has been weighed in the balances of the most excellent Court of Justice of the Italians, it deserves to be called Curial. But it seems mere trifling to say that it has been weighed in the balances of the most excellent Court of Justice of the Italians, because we have no (Imperial) Court of Justice. To this the answer is easy. For, though we have no Court of Justice in Italy in the sense of the one (Supreme) Court of the King of Germany, still the members of such a Court are not wanting. And just as the members of the German Court are united under one Prince, so the members of ours have been united by the gracious light of Reason. Wherefore, it would be false to assert that the Italians have no such Court of Justice, though we have no Prince, because we have a Court, though, as a body, it is scattered.[1]

This takes us beyond our brief. 'Curial' seems to mean 'judicious', and the passage seems to be Dante's way of insisting that to attain this pure diction is a moral achievement, a product of integrity and equilibrium in the poet, in some sense, perhaps, a manifestation of the Aristotelean mean.

Book II is of less interest, chiefly because we feel here the lack of the Book III and Book IV which were planned but never written. This is especially true of

[1] *De Vulgari Eloquentia*, pp. 41, 42.

chapters ii and iv, in which Dante begins to sketch a
structure of distinction by genres:

> Next, we ought to possess a sound judgment as to those things
> which suggest themselves to us as fit to be uttered, so as to decide
> whether they ought to be sung in the way of Tragedy, Comedy,
> or Elegy. By Tragedy we understand the Higher Style, by
> Comedy, the Intermediate Style, by Elegy we understand the
> Lower style. If our subject appears fit to be sung in the Tragic
> style we must then assume the Illustrious Vulgar Tongue, and
> consequently we must write a properly constructed *Canzone*. If
> it appears fit to be sung in the Comic style, sometimes the Illus-
> trious and sometimes the Lower Vulgar Tongue should be used,
> and the judgment to be exercised in this case we reserve for treat-
> ment in the Fourth book. If our subject appears fit to be sung
> in the Elegiac style we must adopt the Lower Vulgar Tongue
> alone.[1]

This, which explains, of course, what Dante meant by
the title "The Divine Comedy", is plainly his version of
the distinction made by Puttenham and other Elizabethans between the high or lofty, the mean, and the
base styles. That distinction strikes us now as mere
pedantry and there is some reason for arguing that it
was made only to be blurred almost at once, by Donne.
And yet it dies hard. The three styles, lofty, mean and
base, or sublime, familiar and pathetic, are still, I would
guess, a governing factor in the activity of the practising
poet. It is notable, for instance, that J. M. Synge, when
he had to write of poetic diction, was forced into a
distinction very like that between the sublime and the
pathetic; and Miss Rosemund Tuve claims to find the
distinction maintained in practice by W. B. Yeats. All
the same, it is perhaps as well that we are in no danger

[1] *De Vulgari Eloquentia*, pp. 55, 56.

of finding these difficult questions of tone reduced once more to a hard and fast system. But what emerges from this examination is a substantial identity of outlook, as to poetic diction, in Dante and Dr. Johnson and certain modern poets. One may go further indeed, and speak of a consistent doctrine in this matter shared by all these writers. I suggest that the term is correctly used only when it is used as Dante and Dr. Johnson used it. In other words, the most important question to be asked of any poetic diction concerns its purity or impurity. And that is a question which is never or very seldom asked by modern critics.

VII

"TO SPEAK BUT WHAT WE UNDERSTOOD"

WHEN Mr. Eliot asserted that "to have the virtues of good prose is the first and minimum requirement of great poetry", he was echoing Ezra Pound, who was in turn repeating what he had learnt from Ford Madox Ford. If we read the poetry of these three writers we can see them trying to practise what they preach; in some sense therefore their poetry exhibits a renewed drawing together of prosaic and poetic language. And yet we cannot deny that in some other respects their poetry exhibits language removed further than ever before from prosaic discipline. When all is said and done, "Little Gidding" is less prosaic than "The Vanity of Human Wishes". Mr. Eliot, therefore, does not mean all that he seems to say.

In what sense, then, are we to understand him? To put it another way, what is the gulf that remains to be bridged, after all the compliments to "The Vanity of Human Wishes", between Augustan and contemporary verse?

Historically, of course, the gulf that yawns is the tradition of Romantic poetry. Both T. S. Eliot and Ezra Pound have freely acknowledged their debts to this tradition, especially in its final phase as "Symbolism"; and it is there that we must seek for whatever it is that draws their poetry away from prose, while their other allegiances draw these together.

To explain this, we must return to an earlier stage of our argument (p. 27, footnote), where we considered Dr. Leavis' objection that the poetry of "Ash Wednesday" has not, after all, 'the virtues of good prose'. In a line such as 'The infirm glory of the positive hour', one sees, it is true, the lexicographer's weighing of the epithet, the prosaic exactness which Mr. Eliot has admired in Johnson. But, as Dr. Leavis points out, such prosaic features are only incidental to a poem which, in its total structure, is as far as possible from the procedure of prose.

At that earlier point we were able to turn the force of this criticism by pointing to a passage from "Little Gidding", in which syntax, no less than vocabulary, was employed with more rigour and subtlety than is usual in all but the best prose. But this stratagem, which sufficed us then, can do so no longer. For five minutes spent on "Little Gidding" will show that this, no less than "Ash Wednesday", is a poem in the symbolist tradition, a poem which works by the arrangement of images, letting the meaning flower unstated, as it were, from the space between them. It follows, I think, that dislocation of syntax is essential to all poems written in this tradition. And this is less apparent in "Little Gidding" only because, in respect of that poem, the word 'image' must be given the very widest meaning, so as to comprehend whole substantial blocs of verse. The whole of the passage we quoted ('There are three conditions which often look alike') is, from this point of view, a single 'image', and in the massive scheme of "Little Gidding" as a whole, or "The Four Quartets" as a whole, it stands to other such images in a relation which is musical, not prosaic. The difference between "Ash Wednesday" and "Little Gidding" is only a difference of scale; in the later poem the poet works with extensive blocs of material, where before he dealt only in snatches of verse. But the relationship between the blocs is the same as that between the snatches; it is symbolist, not syntactical.

So far as I know, Mr. Eliot as critic has never committed himself on this matter of syntax. As usual, we can go to Pound to find a principle common to both poets pushed explicitly to its logical conclusion:

A people that grows accustomed to sloppy writing is a people in process of losing grip on its empire and on its itself. And this looseness and blowsiness is not anything as simple and scandalous as abrupt and disordered syntax.

It concerns the relation of expression to meaning. Abrupt and disordered syntax can be at times very honest, and an elaborately constructed sentence can be at times merely an elaborate camouflage.[1]

With this no one can quarrel. But the observation occurs so often in Pound's writing that we have to suspect he means more than he says. We are told so often that we can do without syntax that we begin to think we can do better without it. And there is no doubt that this is what the writer means. It is on this count, for instance, that he prefers Confucius to Aristotle:

As working hypothesis say that Kung is superior to Aristotle by totalitarian instinct. His thought is never something scaled off the surface of facts. It is root volition branching out, the ethical weight is present in every phrase.

[1] *A B C of Reading*, p. 86.

The chief justice had to think more soberly than the tutor and lecturer.

Give the Greek points on explanatory elaborations. The explicitness, that is literally the unfoldedness, may be registered better in the Greek syntax, but the loss must be counted.[1]

It is clear that in Pound's view when the loss is counted, it will more than counterbalance the gain in 'unfoldedness'. In military language, syntax is 'expendable'. So far as this writer can see, it is more of a hindrance than a help; and this explains his affection for the Chinese ideogram. Only an Orientalist can decide whether Fenollosa and Pound are right about the nature of the Chinese written character. But one sees plainly enough, from Pound's own observations and examples, the connection which existed for him between the ideogram and the symbolist aesthetic. The ideogram, as he saw it, was made up out of several radical signs, each standing for a concrete particular. The sign for 'tree', the sign for 'grass', the sign for 'man', the sign for 'sea' are arranged, it seems, in such a way as to make a wall round a mental space wherein is the meaning of the whole. An arrangement of signs makes the meaning of an ideogram as an arrangement of symbols makes the meaning of a symbolist poem. The *Guide to Kulchur* attempts to use the ideogram in prose as the 'Cantos' do in verse. To Ezra Pound questions of language were central to all human experience; and so this train of thought about syntax finds its counterpart in his ethics. It goes very deep indeed. But it is enough for the moment to point out that when Pound tells the poet he must compete with Flaubert, he is far from thinking

[1] *Guide to Kulchur*, p. 279.

94

in the first place about Flaubert's syntax. Indeed he is thinking of just that element in prose fiction (when he speaks of prose he means nearly always novelist's prose), which in the end led him to abandon syntax altogether; he is thinking of the great novelist's terseness and precision in rendering a feature of experience in all its concreteness. He is thinking, in fact, of the novelist's achievement in rendering the image with clean edges and hard colours, all that he himself had striven for in his Imagist phase; he is not thinking at all of the novelist's practice of relating those features by way of syntax.

Pound, then, while he exhorts the poet to learn from the prose-writer, exhorts him no less to avoid prose syntax. On the other hand, there are poets who argue that poetry is vastly different from prose at the same time as they take it for granted that poetry and prose use the same syntax:

> Both employ the same words, *the same syntax*,[1] the same sounds and tones—though differently arranged and differently stimulated. What separates prose from poetry is the difference of those associated relationships which are for ever coming into being and passing away within our psychological and nervous constitution—even though the *elements* which compose the raw material of these activities may be identical. That is why we must be careful never to apply to poetry the same kind of reasoning that we apply to prose. What may be true of one may, quite easily, be utterly without meaning when sought in the other.[2]

This seems, at first blush, to contradict all that has been

[1] My italics.
[2] Paul Valéry, "Poetry and Abstract Thought", tr. Gerard Hopkins, *Essays on Language and Literature*, ed. Hevesi, p. 97.

said about the need for the poet to learn from prose-usage. But it need not do so, and there is nothing in this passage to which Mr. Eliot, at least, could not subscribe. Nothing, indeed, could be better, as defining the relationship to prose of certain parts of "Little Gidding", than to say, as Valéry does, that they exhibit 'the same syntax . . . though differently arranged'.

And yet the passage is ambiguous. When Valéry asserts that the 'raw material' of prose and of poetry is one and the same, he may be agreeing with all that Dr. Johnson thought about the necessity of prosaic discipline in poetry; or he may agree with none of it. For what are the 'elements' of language? Where do they end, and where does 'arrangement' begin? It is plain that 'syntax' is not an element of language in the sense in which 'sounds and tones' are elements. And after all what is syntax but arrangement? The sense of the passage is not far to seek. It is to be found of course in Valéry's practice as a poet. And on that showing there is nothing to disprove the contention that dislocation of syntax is the essential secret of symbolist technique. For even where the forms of prose syntax are retained, it does not follow that the syntax is prose syntax; for concepts may be related in formally correct syntax when the relationship between them is not really syntactical at all, but musical, when words and phrases are notes in a melody, not terms in an ordered statement.

I would guess that English poets are led to acknowledge their duty to purify the language, where French poets are not, because in France the prose-writer does this job where the English prose-writer notoriously scamps it. Because in England the prose-stylist is usually 'poetical', the poet has to become 'prosaic'. However this may be, it seems plain that the contemporary poet cannot, after all, agree with the late-Augustan poet about the relation of prose to poetry. It may be already too late for poetry to revert to the pre-symbolist attitude to syntax. For there are undoubtedly compensations to be derived from the dislocation of syntax, though they may not be those which, according to Mr. Pound, overweighed the absence of the Aristotelean 'unfolded-ness'. To dislocate syntax in the symbolist manner undoubtedly makes possible an unprecedented concentration of one kind of poetic pleasure. Less certainly it may, as certain of its adherents claim, provide for the communication of experiences too tenuous, fugitive or rarefied to be expressed in any of the older ways. On the other hand, it may be doubted whether, unless syntax reappears in our poetry, we can say of it, as Bernard Manning says of Wesley's hymns, that "congregations bred on such stuff should not suffer from flabbiness of thought". For 'congregations' read 'publics'; and it will be doubtful whether after all Mr. Eliot has purified the language as Dr. Johnson did, or whether any poet in the symbolist tradition can do so. Finally, of course, one cannot avoid the fact that the poet's churches are empty, and the strong suspicion that dislocation of syntax has much to do with it. After all, there is no denying that modern poetry is obscure and that it would be less so if the poets adhered to the syntax of prose.

Changes in linguistic habit are related to changes in man's outlook and hence, eventually, to changes in human conduct. Language does not merely reflect such changes; a change in language may precede the other changes, and even help to bring them about. To abandon syntax in poetry is not to start or indulge a literary fashion; it is to throw away a tradition central to human thought and conduct, as to human speech. Pound, at least, knew this and realized what he was doing. He discusses Erigena's remark that "Authority is the possession of right reason":

You may assert in vindication of values registered in idiom itself that the man who 'isn't all there' has only a partial existence. But we are by that time playing with language? as valuable as playing tennis to keep oneself limber.

Even Erigena's dictum can be examined. Authority can in material or savage world come from accumulated prestige based on intuition. We have trust in a man because we have come to regard him (in his entirety) as sapient and well-balanced. We play his hunch. We make an act of faith. But this is not what Erigena meant, and in any case it does not act in contradiction to his statement, but only as an extension of it.

Shakespeare gets ᴛᴏ the far orientals because he does not shut his meaning into egg-shells. Or at least . . . picked up I can't remember where . . . the memory of an oriental viva voce defending Shakespeare's formlessness on the ground that he reached out and merged into nature.

One is here on very dangerous ground. The ideogram is in some way so much more definite, despite its root filaments, than a shell-case definition.[1]

One has to quote at some length, in order to consider more than one component of the 'prose ideogram'. The components here are on the one hand, certain observations about language, on the other, observations about political conduct. It may be, as Pound says, that

[1] *Guide to Kulchur*, pp. 165, 166.

the relationship between these components can be truthfully expressed only as he has expressed it, 'in ideogram', but at least we can see that, in grasping what is common to them, we go to the heart of Pound's dilemma. By hunting his own sort of 'definiteness' (truth only in the particular) he is led to put his trust not in human institutions but in individuals. Similarly he pins his faith on individual words, grunts, broken phrases, half-uttered exclamations (as we find them in the Cantos), on speech atomized, all syllogistic and syntactical forms broken down. Hence his own esteem of the definite lands him at last in yawning vagueness, the 'intuitive' welcome to Mussolini (he 'plays his hunch'), or, elsewhere in *Guide to Kulchur*, the 'intuitive' perception of form as something over and above pigment, stone, chords, and notes, phrases and words.

It would be too much to say that this is the logical end of abandoning prose syntax. But at least the development from imagism in poetry to fascism in politics is clear and unbroken. From a similar conviction about language and poetry Eliot has developed, not quite so obviously, to Royalism and Anglo-Catholicism. And yet it is impossible not to trace a connection between the laws of syntax and the laws of society, between bodies of usage in speech and in social life, between tearing a word from its context and choosing a leader out of the ruck. One could almost say, on this showing, that to dislocate syntax in poetry is to threaten the rule of law in the civilized community.

Once one has seen this connection between law in language and law in conduct, observations about the nature of language take on an awful importance, and one comes to see potential dangers in attitudes which seemed innocuous. Paul Valéry, for instance, seems almost excessively aware of his responsibilities towards language when he begins a discussion by 'cleansing the verbal situation'. And there is truth in the analogy he draws, between choosing a form of words to express a personal insight and casting a vote in party politics:

> None of the available programmes ever fits precisely the needs of our temperament or the nature of our interests. By the mere fact of choosing one of them we gradually become the kind of man who fits the one particular set of proposals and the one particular party.[1]

But since he himself invites the political parallel, we have a right to ask him to pursue it. What, in these circumstances, is the rational course to take? Should one stand as an Independent? Should one refuse to use one's vote at all? Should one pin one's faith on an individual, a leader, and 'play his hunch'? Or should one merely choose as best one can, and not cast one's vote carelessly? In terms of language should one construct a private language? Should one trust the word and distrust the syntax, as Pound does? Or should one scrutinize accepted meanings and choose among them with all possible nicety?

Valéry does not answer these questions, but gives another metaphor instead. He remarks that a word such as 'Time' when 'used in the ordinary course of communication', is for the most part manageable; but can 'become almost magically embarrassing' when withdrawn from circulation and considered by itself.

---

[1] Valéry, *op. cit.* p. 72.

Language, then, he says, is like a plank across a crevasse, which will bear a man provided he does not loiter, or else like an issue of bank-notes:

> Those pieces of paper have passed through many hands. . . . But words, too, have passed through many mouths, have formed part of many phrases, have been so used and abused that only the most meticulous precautions will save us from falling into mental confusion, caught between what we think, or try to think, and what the dictionary, the tribe of authors, and, in general, the rest of mankind, have been striving, ever since the dawn of language, to make us think.[1]

This again is true, but perverse; for it seeks the more recondite difficulties and ignores those which are obvious. For if it is true that a word is a plank on which we must not loiter, may we assume that across a given crevasse there is nothing to choose between one plank or another? Or, if words are dirty notes, should it not be the first of our 'meticulous precautions' to see if the note is for ten shillings or a pound? To Valéry, we observe, the lexicographer is the enemy of the poet, whereas to Pound or Eliot, when they talk of Johnson, he is the natural ally. So he was in the seventeenth century:

> Since then, he made our language pure and good,
> And us to speak but what we understood,
> We owe this praise to him, that should we join
> To pay him, he were paid but with the coin
> Himself hath minted, which we know by this,
> That no words pass for current now but his.
> And though he in a blinder age could change
> Faults to perfections, yet 'twas far more strange

[1] Valéry, *op. cit.* p. 75.

To see (however times, and fashions frame)
His wit and language still remain the same
In all men's mouths; grave preachers did it use
As golden pills, by which they might infuse
Their heavenly physic; ministers of state
Their grave dispatches in his language wrate;
Ladies made curt'sies in them, courtiers legs,
Physicians bills;—perhaps, some pedant begs
He may not use it, for he hears 'tis such,
As in few words a man may utter much.[1]
Could I have spoken in his language too,
I had not said so much, as now I do,
To whose clear memory I this tribute send,
Who dead's my Wonder, living was my Friend.[2]

It is true that ideas of lexicography have changed, and the dictionary is now expected to record usage, not to establish a standard of propriety. But there is no room for any sort of dictionary in the poet's library so long as we believe with Valéry, that, since words are planks on which we must not loiter, "we understand others . . . we understand *ourselves*, by not *dwelling on our words*". From this point of view, for 'us to speak but what we understood', we ought to have given no thought to what we were saying.

This is, perhaps, to bear too hard on what is no more than a graceful paradox. There is a notable absence, in Valéry's writing as in Eliot's, of that 'ethical weight' which Pound esteemed in others, and which we may notice in him. But for all these important differences of

---

[1] An interesting example of the intimate connection between a pure diction and the 'strength' which is concentration and economy. See *ante*, pp. 62-68.

[2] Sir John Beaumont, "To the memory of him who can never be forgotten, Master Benjamin Jonson".

tone, the three poets drive to the same conclusion. For Valéry's solution to the difficulties of communication is to draw a distinction, "when dealing with intellectual problems, between those that I have constructed for myself, those that express some genuine need felt by my mind, and those that are really only the problems of other people".[1] This is the same distinction as that made by Pound when he says "The chief justice had to think more soberly than the tutor or lecturer", and so goes on to dismiss the Greek syntax as a world well lost. Valéry, like Pound, judges an argument not by its coherence but by the weight of personal experience behind it; and to him, no doubt, as to Pound, syntax is a concession to coherence and a betrayal of the "unsophisticated impulses and images which make up the raw material of my personal needs, my personal experience".

He looks at poems in the same way:

I am inclined, personally, to pay much more attention to the formulation and composition of a work of art than to the work itself, and it is my habit, which amounts almost to a mania, to appreciate such works only in terms of the activity that produces them.[2]

For a poet to make such an astonishing admission may be regarded as a *trahison des clercs* on the grand scale. Yet it is not without parallel; Pasternak, for instance, has declared that "every poem describes its own birth". This attitude produces works of which one can say, as I have said of "The Prelude", that at no point do we move out of the poet's mind into the poem. And Mark

---

[1] Valéry, *op. cit.* p. 75.   [2] *Ibid.* p. 93.

van Doren is probably right when he maintains that
"The Prelude" is the first of such poems. Pound's
"Cantos" are of this kind. This poem is at once licenti-
ously formless and austerely formal; for, as Yeats noted
of the early "Cantos", they go towards a poem which
shall stand or fall as a whole, from which no part can
be extracted, quoted, and argued over in itself. In that
sense Pound's poem constitutes the most elaborately
'made thing' that modern poetry has yet seen. And yet
this made thing, this artifact, is not the poem, the made
thing, that Sidney conceived of, not a poem as even
"The Vanity of Human Wishes" is, something standing apart from and independent of its maker. For it
invites, as "The Prelude" does, the admiring reflection,
"What an interesting mind he has"; not that older
reaction, "What an interesting thing to say".[1]

It seems rather ludicrous to consider a collection of
poems as if it were a substitute for Fowler's *Modern
English Usage*. And yet it was not ludicrous to Sir John
Beaumont. But of course no one will argue that the
poem's existence in this capacity is in any way so important as in its other capacities, as communiqué and
creation, as thing said and thing made. But the three
functions hang together. As the language of poetry
becomes more private and distinctive, the poem becomes less and less a manual of correct usage; but at the
same time it becomes less and less a thing said and a
thing made.

[1] An interesting situation arises when we find, or think we find, a
pre-Wordsworthian poet who meets our post-Wordsworthian expecta-
tions. This is the case of John Donne.

CONCLUSION TO PART I

THIS book is an attempt to arrive at the principles underlying purity of poetic diction in English. It is not a historical survey of all English poetry that achieves or attempts such purity. I have taken most of my examples from the most obvious field, where such purity was most to be expected, in certain poetry of the eighteenth century. Though I have found examples in other periods, I am in no position to establish a standard for them, as I have tried to do for part of the eighteenth century. And I might have to modify my account even of the principles, if I had looked, from this point of view, at the difficult case of Milton, for example. Still, I am fairly confident that the principles governing this sort of writing are such as I have described.

At many stages in this enquiry I have been glad of the guidance of Mr. T. S. Eliot, whether as critic or poet. It is part of his achievement, I think, that he has renovated in practice some of the principles I have grouped together under the heading of 'pure diction'. On the other hand, as I have tried to show in the last chapter, he has adopted only some of those principles, not all of them. It may be that he has done all that was practicable and renovated only so much as is appropriate to the present day. At any rate there are many other sides to what he has done, and indeed the other sides have been acknowledged more widely. Just for that reason, and because Mr. Eliot's criticism has always been occasional, not systematic, many critics have invoked his authority for views of poetry which are as different as possible from mine. For that matter, I put forward no personal systematic view of poetry as a whole, but only of one kind of poetry which seems to me to have been neglected. There can be no question of my attacking the systems of others in order to erect my own. I can think of influential critics who have neglected what I will call for the moment my kind of poetry, but who would have no difficulty in fitting it into the systems they have erected or the views they hold. The case is rather different, however, with critics who go out of their way to deny it any status as poetry at all. And it is especially confusing when for their views they invoke the authority of Mr. Eliot no less than I have done for mine.

This is the case, for instance, with Mr. Cleanth Brooks:

T. S. Eliot has commented upon "that perpetual slight alteration of language, words perpetually juxtaposed in new and sudden combinations", which occurs in poetry. It *is* perpetual; it cannot be kept out of the poem; it can only be directed and controlled. The tendency of science is necessarily to stabilize terms, to freeze them into strict denotations; the poet's tendency is by contrast disruptive. The terms are continually modifying each other, and thus violating their dictionary meanings. To take a very simple example, consider the adjectives in the first lines of Wordsworth's evening sonnet: *beauteous, calm, free, holy, quiet, breathless.* The juxtapositions are hardly startling; and yet notice this: the evening is like a nun breathless with adoration. The adjective 'breathless' suggests tremendous excitement; and yet the evening is not only quiet but calm. There is no final contradiction, to be sure; it is *that* kind of calm and *that* kind of excitement, and the two states may well occur together. But the poet has no one term. Even if he had a polysyllabic technical term, the term would not provide the solution for his problem. He must work by contradiction and qualification.[1]

There is no getting round this. Mr. Brooks says as plainly as possible that the poet must never use one word where two will do. And so there can be no room in his view of poetry for the exactness, the economy and the concentration which go with the 'strength' of a pure diction. Where there is such head-on collision as this, there is not much point in arguing the matter. I think Mr. Brooks is wrong, and that his view of poetry pushes to the extreme some quite common ideas which will drive the poet further than ever into a private wilderness and alienate more and more potential readers.

For it is, after all, to the would-be poet of to-day that I should like to address myself. I hope that no one who reads this book will see in it only a Quixotic preference for the pedestrian and the prosaic in English poetry. I readily admit the existence of some English poetry which is prosaic in this bad sense; many poems by John Byrom are of this sort. And on the other hand such a high-flown poem as Yeats' "Ribh at the Tomb of Baile and Ailinn" is prosaic in the sense that it has 'the virtues of good prose'.

It is now several years since the most eminent of living English poets looked forward to a recrudescence of poetic diction in contemporary writing. I should like to think that this study might help some practising poet to a poetry of urbane and momentous statement.

[1] *The Well Wrought Urn*, pp. 8 and 9.

PART II

DICTION AND INVENTION: A VIEW
OF WORDSWORTH

Wordsworth was his own worst critic. Coleridge was right. The Preface to *Lyrical Ballads* is great literature; but it is great as a personal testament, not as criticism, or if as criticism then criticism at its most theoretical. It is not theoretical in the sense that Wordsworth did not know from personal experience what he was talking about. He did, of course; that is what is meant by calling it a testament. It is theoretical in the sense that it is wise about the nature and the function of poetry and poetic pleasure, and foolish about poetic techniques.

To be particular, Wordsworth invites us to approach his poems by considering their diction; whereas most of those poems by-pass questions of diction altogether. For the question of diction only arises when a poem begs it. It is never perhaps indifferent, but it is often of little importance. In the eighteenth century this was generally acknowledged; Goldsmith, for instance, says that a chaste diction is less important in the sublime poem than in the pathetic. And it is notable that modern poets when they have approached the question have been forced to the same distinction.[1] We may well be reluctant to reopen an old controversy which proved so often sterile; but we need 'sublime', or something like it, to classify the many poems which merely avoid questions of diction altogether.

[1] J. M. Synge, Preface to *Poems and Translations*.

We can do so sufficiently for the present purpose by exhuming another critical term which has fallen into disuse. I mean the notion of 'invention', or finding. There are poems which are poetic by virtue of the finding and conduct of a fable, over and above the poetry of their language. I am well aware of the dangers of this contention. It is always dangerous to divorce poetry from words and locate it in some air-drawn 'form'. Nevertheless, T. Sturge Moore is an example of the poet whose language is undistinguished, whose powers of invention, at least in his longer works, are strikingly poetic. We can call a poem 'sublime' when it displays powers of invention so conspicuously that considerations of diction, while never indifferent, are of only minor moment.

Now Wordsworth is a conspicuous example of a poet in whom invention is so powerful that diction hardly ever matters. De Quincey said as much in a fine passage[1] when he hailed Wordsworth as above all a discoverer of new or forgotten truths. And of no part of Wordsworth's work is this so true as of *Lyrical Ballads*. Wordsworth was technically incompetent at least until 1801, when he seems to have put himself to school with Chaucer, Shakespeare and Milton. By luck or genius (they amount to the same thing) he had before that hit upon some primitive forms which could just sustain what he had to say; and what he had found to say before that was so novel and surprising that it could carry the day. Even "The Brothers" and "Michael" are great in spite of, not because of, their

[1] *De Quincey's Literary Criticism* (ed. Darbishire, 1909), p. 234. Quoted *post*, p. 193.

language. And even so, luck failed him on occasions; for instance "The Two Thieves" of 1800 displays a nobly poetical conception (similar to "The Old Cumberland Beggar") thrown away in an inappropriate form. The early poems, when they succeed, do so by virtue of invention; the language is as nearly irrelevant as it can be in poetry.

After the turn of the century Wordsworth emerges, through some uncomfortable experiments, as a highly accomplished poet. He creates not one style, but many, according to what he needs to do. There is the style of the political sonnets; the style of "The Prelude"; and the style of the Immortality Ode. There are others, but these are the most important. And each of these styles can be called a 'diction', in the sense of a private language, a distinctive vocabulary and turn of phrase. Wordsworth's own criticism had paved the way for this loose usage. And the shift in meaning is further obscured for us by the circumstance that some later poets, such as Arnold, made use of one or other of the Wordsworthian styles; so that we detect 'Wordsworthian diction' in other poets.

But this use of diction, to mean a private language, is the very opposite of the older one, by which it was 'the perfection of a common language'. It is only the latter of which one can say that it is pure or impure. And this is a diction which hardly ever appears in Wordsworth's work. The question of purity does not arise. Almost to the end what matters in Wordsworth is his invention, his astonishing discoveries about human sentiments. As he pieced his discoveries together into systems, he had to learn his trade and master techniques more elaborate and sophisticated than those which had served him in *Lyrical Ballads*. But at no time does the question of pure or impure diction enter into the matter.

After all, how could it? A pure diction embodies urbanity; a vicious diction offers to do that, and fails. But Wordsworth was not interested in urbanity, and had no faith in it; he pledged himself to its opposite, a determined provincialism. He spoke as a solitary, not as a spokesman; urbanity was none of his business, nor diction either. It is one way of explaining what went wrong with Wordsworth's poetry, in his later life, to say that as recognition came to him, he saw himself more and more as, after all, a spokesman of national sentiment.[1] No poet was less fitted, by training and temperament, for such a role; and no poet's art was so unsuitable for carrying it.

There are two or three exceptions. The most important is "The White Doe of Rylstone". It is a poem which will never be popular, because it does without so many attractions incidental and usual in poetry. Alone of all Wordsworth's poems, it requires of the reader that he come to terms with the famous contention that "There neither is, nor can be, any essential difference between the language of prose and of metrical composition". In the Preface to *Lyrical Ballads*, Wordsworth's views on diction are so ill considered that, to the reader baffled by "The White Doe of

---

[1] Quite early in Wordsworth's career he began to produce patriotic sonnets on the Miltonic model, in which he aimed to express national sentiment. Some of these are widely admired; but it is an enthusiasm which I cannot share.

Rylstone", they can still give little assistance. But they are far more pertinent to that poem than to any of the ballads.

The verse-form of "The White Doe" has been variously defined as derived from Scott and from Virgil. More probably, I think, the model was Samuel Daniel. A prefatory note to "Yarrow Visited" implies that Wordsworth read Daniel about the time he was reading Chaucer, soon after the turn of the century. Now Daniel was the poet selected by Coleridge, when he discussed Wordsworth's style, to exemplify the genuinely and culpably prosaic in verse:

> Ten Kings had from the Norman Conqu'ror reign'd
> With intermix'd and variable fate,
> When England to her greatest height attain'd
> Of power, dominion, glory, wealth, and state;
> After it had with much ado sustain'd
> The violence of princes, with debate
> For titles and the often mutinies
> Of nobles for their ancient liberties.

> For first, the Norman, conqu'ring all by might,
> By might was forced to keep what he had got;
> Mixing our customs and the form of right
> With foreign constitutions, he had brought;
> Mast'ring the mighty, humbling the poorer wight,
> By all severest means that could be wrought;
> And, making the succession doubtful, rent
> His new-got state, and left it turbulent.

These are two of the stanzas quoted from Daniel by Coleridge; and it would be hard to find in English poetry another passage so similar as this from "The White Doe":

It was the time when England's Queen
Twelve years had reigned, a Sovereign dread;
Nor yet the restless crown had been
Disturbed upon her virgin head;
But now the inly-working North
Was ripe to send its thousands forth,
A potent vassalage, to fight
In Percy's and in Neville's right,
Two earls fast leagued in discontent,
Who gave their wishes open vent;
And boldly urged a general plea,
The rites of ancient piety
To be triumphantly restored,
By the stern justice of the sword!
And that same Banner, on whose breast
The blameless Lady had exprest
Memorials chosen to give life
And sunshine to a dangerous strife;
That Banner, waiting for the Call,
Stood quietly in Rylstone-hall.

It seems likely that those who dislike "The White Doe"
as prosaic can call upon the authority of Coleridge.

And yet the comparison is unjust. For if Wordsworth's verse has 'the virtues of good prose' (as Daniel's
has), it has also a felicitous concentration that can only
be called poetic. That Wordsworth's account of the
reasons for the Rising of the North should tally with
the findings of modern historians is interesting, but
not so important as the consistency and conciseness of
his treatment. A modern editor[1] has drawn attention
to the propriety of 'inly-working', pithily characteriz-
ing the complicated discontents which were at work.

[1] Comparetti, "The White Doe of Rylstone" (*Cornell Studies in English*, xxix).

Dynastic and personal quarrels lay behind the insurrection and were the cause of it at least as much as the stubborn adherence to the Old Faith. Wordsworth's acknowledgment of this colours his whole treatment, and gives an ironic aptness, for instance, to his account of the banner. Embroidered with the Cross and the wounds of Christ, it was to give 'life and sunshine to a dangerous strife'; 'sunshine' is played off against the 'inly-working', expressing the symbolic with the actual function of the flag, and throwing on the whole enterprise the shadow of divided loyalties and coming doom. More, the theme of the whole poem, the hard-won serenity of the abandoned lady, symbolized in her creature, the doe, is an example of just such 'inly-working'.

In the verse of "The White Doe of Rylstone", Wordsworth achieved, as nowhere else in a poem of any length, a pure diction, a speech of civilized urbanity which can 'purify the language of the tribe'. Of course, the poem exhibits only one mode of such a diction, the mode proper to the peculiar purpose of historical narrative, and to the correspondent tone, neither elevated nor intimate, of the so-called 'mean style'. This is a staple verse and does not lend itself to purple passages, though Coleridge, who thought Wordsworth a poet of purple passages, claimed to find one. Throughout, the verse maintains one level of subdued excellence. There are impurities,[1] but they are few. The verse of "The

---

[1] An example of such 'impurity' may help—lines 720, 721:
  "Like those eight Sons—who, in a ring,
  (Ripe men or blooming in life's spring . . .)".
—where the second line is too 'literary'. Wordsworth tried to change it in 1827, but returned to this version in the 1837 text.

White Doe", a poem which Wordsworth believed to be 'in conception, the highest work he had ever produced', answers to the programme announced in the Preface to *Lyrical Ballads*; but not to the programme which Coleridge would have substituted. It is notable, for instance, that the poem avoids personification and generalization, those components of the diction which Wordsworth rejected. Miss Comparetti has shown that "The White Doe" depends upon an abstraction, upon the 'melancholy', not of Shakespeare and Robert Burton, nor of Matthew Arnold, but of Thomson and Gray, the Miltonic 'melancholy' which is strong and composed. The poem depends on that notion; but, true to his principles, Wordsworth eschews all reference to it as a personified abstraction, and embodies it instead in the symbolic or emblematic figure of 'the doe'. By so doing, he reaped just the benefits which he had promised himself. For Melancholy had been handled so often by the decadent poets of the sensibility-cult that in its form as a personified abstraction it was unmanageable to any serious ends; Wordsworth, adopting a diction which did not permit him to personify, was able to make the Miltonic melancholy once again a respectable topic and a moral force.

I have called the doe 'a symbolic or emblematic figure'. One hesitates to find in the doe the force of a symbol; and yet it is hard to say that it is anything else. Wordsworth was right when he compared it with the 'milk-white lamb' in "The Faerie Queene". "The White Doe" is a thoroughly Spenserian poem. For all the great difference between Spenser's opulent rhetoric and the sobriety of Wordsworth's language, although the structure has none of Spenser's complexity, although Wordsworth does not think in Spenser's terms, we infer a marked similarity between the ways of thought and feeling which produced the two poems. Wordsworth speaks of Una's lamb as 'that emblem'; and there is no need to quarrel about terms. If the doe is symbolic, it is so as Una's lamb is, or Dryden's hind, or the statue of Hermione in *The Winter's Tale*. These figures seem to arise from conceptions dwelt upon so intently that they assume at last a wraith-like substance and life. They are quite different from such recognized 'symbols' as Perdita-Marina, the girl lost and found, or Blake's Little Boy Lost, or Wordsworth's own man upon the moor who stands or strides or sits, wreathed in mist, through poem after poem. These others are the images which walk about the poet's mind, asking to be explained. The poetry which uses them is a poetry of wise passiveness; the poetry which uses symbols of the other kind is a work of will, of contrivance and persistence, not a finding but a making.

The poem cannot be appreciated until we realize this effort of will behind it, and the internal tension which that produces. On a first reading it appears innocent of compression, concentration, contrast or irony. There seems to be no tension, whether in the eddying narrative or the fluent language. This impression must persist until the reader can cultivate an ear or a palate for diction, for a central purity; then the tension appears, in our awareness of the words that have been left out. Because the tone is less elevated, it is easy to miss the point that the poem is written in a choice language, as "The Deserted Village" is, or "The

Task". Once we appreciate that, the poem takes its place in the line of activity inaugurated by the "Ode to Duty", or, even earlier, in "Resolution and Independence". In these poems Wordsworth acknowledges that the first springs of his creativeness have dried up, and that what comes after can be no longer buoyant with invention, with new discoveries given, but must be worked for, with self-discipline. At least, this is the implication for his art of the changes Wordsworth announces in his morality. Will and duty are to take the place of idleness and spontaneity. Perhaps Wordsworth misjudged the situation or his own temperament: at any rate the new programme was much poorer than the old one, from the point of view of the poems it produced; and one is inclined to agree with Dr. Leavis that "The Wordsworth who in the 'Ode to Duty' spoke of the 'genial sense of youth' as something he happily surrendered had seen the hiding-places of his power close".[1] But "The White Doe of Rylstone" seems to me one poem in which the new programme justified itself. The heroine is herself the embodiment of resolution, endurance, and the will kept at a stretch: for all her exclusively passive role (here is the paradox, the pathos, and most of the interest), the lady, by embracing that role as a duty, makes of it something active, resolute and noble. This is Wordsworth's original and compelling variation on the theme of Miltonic melancholy. And apart from this, regarded from the poet's point of view, "The White Doe" itself is similarly an achievement of resolution, effort and self-denying endurance. It is the most absolutely 'made'

[1] *Revaluation*, p. 183.

thing that Wordsworth ever produced. It is free-standing, in its own right; not, like "The Prelude" or, to a lesser degree, "The Excursion", taking half of its strength along the cord which still connects the poem to its parent. "The White Doe" is impersonal and self-contained, thrown free of its creator with an energy he never compassed again. He tried again, but with little success, in "Laodamia".

COLERIDGE AND IMPROVISED DICTION

YOUR poem must eternal be,
  Dear Sir! it cannot fail!
For 'tis incomprehensible,
  And without head or tail.

Thus Coleridge, "To the author of 'The Ancient Mariner'". It is a silly rhyme, for "The Ancient Mariner" has both head and tail, and in fact is one of the best constructed poems of the Romantic Revival. The architectural analogy is out of fashion; and 'construction' and 'form' have been suspect in criticism since 1928:

Construction, Design, Form, Rhythm, Expression . . . are more often than not mere *vacua* in discourse, for which a theory of criticism should provide explainable substitutes.[1]

I am not aware that the substitutes have appeared. A poem exists in printed space and reading time, and with some poems we feel that the space and time they occupy are not chosen at random, but are exactly or nearly right, or too little, or too much. We may feel further that the several components of a poem are given too much or too little room, as when we say that the stanza chosen is too short, or that the exposition takes up too much time, or that a theme would be better in another place. "The Ancient Mariner" begs such questions as these, and so one can say that it is well or ill formed, well or badly constructed.

[1] I. A. Richards, *Principles of Criticism*, p. 20.

There are other poems by Coleridge which challenge the same kind of judgment, notably the little haunting allegories such as "Time, Real and Imaginary" and a beautiful love-poem, "The Happy Husband"; but most of his better-known poems evade such questions. They are truly formless, precisely amorphous. And if this amorphousness was deliberate (as I think it was), the poet's intention explains much that is peculiar in his diction.

That the diction is peculiar will hardly be denied:

> Her front sublime and broad,
> Her flexile eyebrows wildly haired and low,
> And her full eye, now bright, now unillumed,
> Spake more than Woman's thought.

These lines are from "The Destiny of Nations", written in 1796, the year before "The Ancient Mariner" and two years after "Lewti". It is certainly a poor poem, but not so poor that we can dismiss the vicious diction as the bungling of one who knew no better. In its very excess, it seems wilful. That, at any rate, was the opinion of C. H. Herford, writing of the "Religious Musings":

And though the manner swells too loftily, partly under the infection of Schiller's *Robbers*, and the style bristles with daring neologisms, marks of the literary rebel, yet the poetic material chaotically strewn on the page is very rich. . . .[1]

The impurity of diction is thrust before our eyes in such words (from "Religious Musings") as 'contemplant', 'operant', 'unsensualized', 'imbreathe', 'twy-streaming', 'rapture-trembling', 'toy-bewitched', 'sure-refuged'. And Coleridge later apologized for his 'profusion of

[1] C. H. Herford, *The Age of Wordsworth*, p. 172.

double epithets', 'general turgidness', 'the swell and glitter both of thought and diction'[1] and 'a too ornate, and elaborately poetic diction'.[2] But the real perversity of the language is only to be seen in the dislocation of normal syntax and word-order, in a style as eccentric as Milton's but less consistent. And it occurs in such a way as to seem (precisely) a perversity, a wilful ugliness, not the simple result of knowing no better.

According to Herford, the piece is not only unchaste but chaotic. And Coleridge admits as much in his title. What is one to make of a poem with a plural title? Is it one thing or several, a cycle or a series? The difficulty is ever-present as one reads Coleridge. "Kubla Khan" is a fragment; "Christabel" a torso; others are better described as 'pieces of poetry' than as 'poems'. Coleridge talks, to himself or to others, and we 'listen in'. In all these cases, I think, we tacitly agree that we are listening to Coleridge talking, not to a poetic statement, but to a section cut from a stream of talk. Coleridge again admitted as much when he called "The Nightingale" a 'conversation-poem'. And in "The Improvisatore", we see the poem actually emerging out of conversation.

In this curious piece, sub-titled "John Anderson, my Jo, John", and in some editions called "New Thoughts on Old Subjects", the Friend is engaged in conversation by two young women and, when fully launched on his stream of discourse, he modulates out of prose into verse. The improviser was a heroic figure of the

---

[1] See Coleridge's Preface to the *Collected Poems*, 1st and 2nd editions.

[2] *Literary Life*, i, 51, quoted as footnote to the Preface.

Romantic movement through Europe. He provides the title for an early novel by Hans Andersen. Mickiewicz was a famous improviser and uses the figure in 'Forefathers' Eve". Pushkin used him elaborately in "Egyptian Nights". He belongs with the Aeolian Harp and the Upas Tree, amid the characteristic furniture of the Romantic Age. He could be used in many ways. He embodied the spontaneity of poetic creation. He strained himself, in inventing against the clock, and so embodied the view of poetry as a sort of painful possession. He was a professional entertainer, and so he could be used, as by Pushkin, to lay bare the relationship between the Romantic poet and his society. In the present connection, what matters most about the cult of the improviser is the most obvious thing about him: he makes it up as he goes along, and 'it', therefore, the thing he makes, is not a poem, a statement, having shape and finality, but a piece of poetry, the record of a visitation, the section of a flow of talk, a spasm or a series of spasms. The poetry which tries to seem improvised will be spasmodic; a consistent tone of discourse will not be wanted in such poetry, any more than the consistent development of a single theme. It follows that, in such poetry, a pure diction will not be merely irrelevant, but positively unwanted.

This is one of the most momentous changes in the history of poetry. It marks the disappearance of the Renaissance conviction about the poem as a made thing, thrown free of its makar, something added to creation and free-standing in its own right. The poet hereafter is legislator, seer, scapegoat and reporter; he is no longer an artificer. And from this time forward 'artificial' is a term of dispraise whereas to Sidney and Puttenham and Gabriel Harvey it had been the highest praise. Now 'artificial' is opposed to 'natural' where before it had belonged with it:

Verum id est maxime naturale, quod fieri natura optime patitur.

This glorification of the natural, and its equation with the spontaneous, the amorphous, the artless and the personal, is still a potent force in the writing and reading of poetry; so much so, that it is still impossible to see this revolution in perspective. Plainly much was lost and something was gained; it is still impossible to balance the profit and loss. Meanwhile, though some poems appeared which were still consummately 'made', the Romantic age is inevitably rich in fragments, pieces of poetry rather than poems, and preludes to poems that were never written. The schoolboy says that the Romantics rebelled against form. He is often corrected —the Romantics, we say, rebelled against certain existent forms, and substituted others of their own. And of course so they did. But the schoolboy is right, all the same; at times the Romantics rebelled not only against the forms they inherited, but against all forms, form as such.

Between amorphous poems and impure diction the connection is obvious. It is one function of a pure diction to maintain a consistent tone of discourse throughout a poem. Where a poem in that sense is not wanted, but only a passage of poetic thought, the diction is wilfully dislocated to mark the spasmodic nature of the whole. We need a complete poem, to see how the two work together:

TO A FRIEND, WHO HAD DECLARED HIS INTENTION
OF WRITING NO MORE POETRY

Dear Charles! whilst yet thou wert a babe, I ween
That Genius plunged thee in that wizard fount
Hight Castalie: and (sureties of thy faith)
That Pity and Simplicity stood by,
And promised for thee, that thou shouldst renounce
The world's low cares and lying vanities,
Steadfast and rooted in the heavenly Muse,
And washed and sanctified to Poesy.
Yes—thou wert plunged, but with forgetful hand
Held, as by Thetis erst her warrior son;
And with those recreant unbaptized heels
Thou'rt flying from thy bounden minist'ries—
So sore it seems and burthensome a task
To weave unwithering flowers! But take thou heed:
For thou art vulnerable, wild-eyed boy,
And I have arrows mystically dipt,
Such as may stop thy speed. Is thy Burns dead?
And shall he die unwept, and sink to earth,
"Without the meed of one melodious tear?"
Thy Burns, and Nature's own beloved bard,
Who to the "Illustrious of his native Land
So properly did look for patronage."
Ghost of Maecenas! hide thy blushing face!
They snatched him from the sickle and the plough—
To gauge ale-firkins.
                        Oh! for shame return!
On a bleak rock, midway the Aonian mount,
There stands a lone and melancholy tree,
Whose aged branches to the midnight blast
Make solemn music: pluck its darkest bough,
Ere yet the unwholesome night-dew be exhaled,
And weeping wreath it round thy Poet's tomb.
Then in the outskirts, where pollutions grow,

> Pick the rank henbane and the dusky flowers
> Of night-shade, or its red and tempting fruit,
> These with stopped nostril and glove-guarded hand
> Knit in nice intertexture, so to twine
> The illustrious brow of Scotch Nobility.

The poem is certainly wayward. Considered as a poem about Burns, it occupies itself for half its length on an introduction to the theme which is no introduction at all since, even after so much, the transition to the name of Burns is very abrupt. Even within that section, there is no connection between the embarrassed Spenserian diction of the opening and the fantastic conceit of the heels by which Charles was dipt in Castaly, as Achilles in another fount by Thetis, and with which he now flies from his duty. But when we reach the end of the paragraph, and the withering contempt in the drop from elevated diction to 'ale-firkins', we realize that the abrupt transitions and the spasmodic development are part and parcel with the veering, swerving tone, and the condition of the poet's achieving the contempt he wants. The same deliberate bathos is contrived to the same effect at the end of the second paragraph. And one is left with the solitary criticism that the convention is not sufficiently established from the first. In other words, the Spenserian diction of the first lines should be even more grotesque than it is.

In the eighteenth century poets had known how to exploit bathos, but never to this effect. Coleridge's bathos has nothing to do with the mock-heroic. He achieves a contempt as withering as Pope's, but by quite different means. And I think it is even more caustic. For Sporus was immortalized; the gentry of the

Caledonian Hunt are dismissed to limbo. Coleridge in fact—it is a commonplace—had to express experiences, thoughts and feelings, for which he could find no room in existent poetic forms. It may be doubted, though, whether some of them could be expressed in poetic form at all, at least if we give any weight to 'form'.

"Dejection" is one of the great poems in the language. It is a true poem, not a piece of poetry, a made thing, not a snatch of talk. And it is no accident that Coleridge in his title should seek the sanction of a traditional form, the Horatian ode. The poem seeks that sanction and obtains it. It came, as we now know, from a harrowing personal predicament; yet the voice which speaks it is impersonal and timeless, the voice of a language, the voice of Man, of no one and everyone. It goes without saying, after this, that the diction is pure. It has none of the characteristic devices, personification and the rest. But the diction is pure as Johnson's is, because it mediates between conversation and rhetoric, and because it embodies an urbanity. The point is made already when we call it impersonal, the voice of a language:

> Well! If the Bard was weather-wise, who made
>   The grand old ballad of Sir Patrick Spence,
>   This night, so tranquil now, will not go hence
>   Unroused by winds, that ply a busier trade
> Than those which mould yon cloud in lazy flakes,
> Or the dull sobbing draft, that moans and rakes
>   Upon the strings of this Eolian lute,
>   Which better far were mute.

This extraordinary sentence achieves in little all that the poem does. It is largely a matter of syntax. The sentence, coiling through eight lines, brings together moods and ideas which would seem incompatible did we not see them living together easily in one logical structure. The first two lines are positively 'jaunty', with a cracked gaiety which only betrays itself five lines later when it breaks into the depression which underlies it. At the same time the external wind and the inward rush of thought come together, not by metaphor nor in the conventional 'Eolian' (for by that time the fusion has happened) but again by syntax. In the same way, and as part of the same process, the near-colloquialism of the first lines moves, not veering abruptly but as if inevitably, into the elevated rhetoric of 'the dull sobbing draft, that moans and rakes Upon the strings'. The two poles of the diction are thus established and the poem slides eloquently between them into the key which is to govern the whole. The struggle with the medium issues in a moral conquest. For the purity thus established is a sign of good breeding, and this is essential to a poem which is to deal in intimate matters, taboo in normal discourse, where the speaker continually skirts self-pity. The diction is sustained and he never steps over; it is permissible to call this a profound urbanity.

"Dejection", then, is a poem consummately 'made', and far from improvisation. Yet one may think that it owes something to the deliberately improvised pieces that stand near to it in the history of Coleridge's verse. The first personal version, printed by Professor de Selincourt, is interesting in this connection, quite apart from its poignancy as a human document. To go no further than the lines quoted, the swiftness of startling transition at the very start of the poem almost certainly owes something to such experiments in abrupt changes of mood and in harsh changes of wilfully eccentric diction. And a conservative can make the point that Coleridge proved himself in the wrong. At least once he found elastic enough those traditional laws of form and diction, and accommodated in them the new experiences which had seemed to demand new forms and new diction, or even the disappearance of form and diction altogether.

Coleridge's experiments in amorphous poetry and dislocated diction can be compared to some purpose with the *tour de force* of Romantic improvisation, "Don Juan". Byron too is the improvisatore and with him, too, the experiment takes the same form, a deliberate courting of impurities in diction:

> He that reserves his laurels for posterity
> > (Who does not often claim the bright reversion)
> Has generally no great crop to spare it, he
> > Being only injured by his own assertion;
> And although here and there some glorious rarity
> > Arise like Titan from the sea's immersion,
> The major part of such appellants go
> To—God knows where—for no one else can know.

"Is there no bright reversion in the sky . . .?" Fragments from Pope gleam, like spars from a shipwrecked world, all about the tumultuous sea of Byron's verse, a criterion acknowledged but no longer to the point, thrown with a sort of desperate jocularity into this poem which veers crazily in rhyme and diction and movement, about the poet's inexhaustible mind. For here the poem as artifact has utterly disappeared. However long we read we are never into the poem and out of the poet's mind. The two have become one, as in "The Prelude".

Byron, of course, 'caught on', as Coleridge never did. And ever since 'urbanity' has meant the manner of Don Juan, an assurance never occupied but only acknowledged as the poet veers past it, a sort of raffish insouciance, above all a pervasive irony. After this a poet can write about nothing, and defend himself with irony. A poet has only one subject—himself. And so long as he quizzes himself, we cannot complain. For this is civilization, maturity, urbanity—the quizzical stance.

Of course this is unfair. It is not so easy to write a poem like "Don Juan". No one has done it since Byron, or not on such a scale. But it is true that the amorphous poem, the improvisation, is drastically limited in tone after "Don Juan". The sublime poems continue. But in poems about human affairs, the Byronic irony is hard to avoid, even to-day. In Coleridge's hands the amorphous poem had a far wider range of mood, but it is a range which we have lost. We can only choose between traditional forms (the diction goes with them) and, on the other hand, a deprecating wit.

III

SHELLEY'S URBANITY

(i) *The Shelleyan Sublime*

However we look at it, Shelley affects the sublime. We may not know what the sublime is, and yet know that, to be acceptable, it must include "The Triumph of Life" and "Prometheus Unbound". Whatever we think of these poems (and the latter at any rate makes dull reading in my experience), there can be no doubt how high the poet aims in them, what large pretensions he makes. In short, whatever his performance, Shelley promises in these poems to move on a level where (for instance) 'urbanity' cannot count.

But this is what makes criticism of Shelley so difficult; he evades so many standards. In this he is peculiar even among the poets of the sublime. His sublimity is peculiarly indefinite and impalpable. From one point of view his poetry is certainly sensuous; but the sensuousness is not of a sort to bring into poetry the reek and grit of common experience. For Shelley goes as far as poetry can go, while it uses intelligible language, in cutting the hawsers which tie his fancies to the ground. His metaphors are tied so tenuously to any common ground in experience that it is peculiarly hard to arrive at their mooring in common logic or association. It was this, for instance, which gave Mr. Eliot so much trouble with an image in "To a Skylark":

> Keen as are the arrows
> Of that silver sphere,
> Whose intense lamp narrows
> In the white dawn clear
> Until we hardly see—we feel that it is there.

It is typical of Shelley's obscurity that as it happens I find no difficulty here, but only the accurate register of a sense-perception[1]—the fading of the morning-star. For Shelley evades as many standards as he can, and when he cannot evade them, makes their application as difficult as he can; or so it must seem to the harrassed critic. And as a result we can expect to find the critics even further than usual from agreement about the nature of his achievement. All one can say is that the period of uncritical adulation is past, and that we have learnt, since Dr. Leavis' damaging scrutiny,[2] to be on our guard when Shelley is most sublime.

At any rate, if Shelley is great, in "Prometheus Unbound", in "The Triumph of Life", even in such shorter poems as "The Cloud", he is so by virtue of *invention*, the characteristic virtue of the sublime. And the eighteenth-century critics would agree that in poems of this sort the poet has considerable licence. We can expect (and it is only right) that the diction of an epic or a hymn will be less chaste than the diction of a familiar epistle. And we can go so far as to say that in the case of such poems the question of diction should not be introduced at all. But this is not quite true.

[1] Cf. from "Ode to Naples":
> "The isle-sustaining ocean-flood,
> A plane of light between two heavens of azure."

[2] *Revaluation*, pp. 203-240.

There are always limits. As Keats remarked, "English must be kept up"—even in the epic. And Shelley as usual goes to the limit, or over it.

"The Cloud" is a good example:

> Sublime on the towers of my skiey bowers,
>   Lightning my pilot sits;
> In a cavern under is fettered the thunder,
>   It struggles and howls at fits;
> Over earth and ocean, with gentle motion,
>   This pilot is guiding me,
> Lured by the love of the genii that move
>   In the depths of the purple sea;
> Over the rills, and the crags, and the hills,
>   Over the lakes and the plains,
> Wherever he dream, under mountain or stream,
>   The Spirit he loves remains;
> And I all the while bask in Heaven's blue smile,
>   Whilst he is dissolving in rains.

The image is audacious to begin with. There is no reason in natural philosophy to give a basis in logic to the notion that a cloud is directed by electric charges. The image depends entirely on association, and the leap of association is something of a strain. However, it is made easier by the elaboration which makes the thunder a prisoner in the dungeons of the cloud. Natural philosophy lends its aid to the logical association of a cloud with the genii of the sea; and the lightning is supposed amorous of the sea—a link sanctioned by neither logic nor association (however 'free'), but carried as it were on the cloud's back. The real difficulty comes with the 'he', appearing three times in the last six lines. Is this 'he' the lightning, the actual cloud, or the idea of the cloud which is always present even in a cloudless sky? We are given no indication that this 'he' is any other than 'the pilot', i.e. the lightning. And yet this is surely impossible in the last two lines:

> And I all the while bask in Heaven's blue smile,
> Whilst he is dissolving in rains.

Shelley means to say, I think, that the ideal cloud continues to bask while the actual cloud dissolves in rains; but in fact he says that the cloud, ideal or actual, rides high, while the lightning dissolves. And this is lunacy.

The fault here lies in the conduct and development of a metaphor, not, in the first place, in choice of language. And yet the two cannot be distinguished since the metaphor only comes to grief on the loose use of a personal pronoun. This looseness occurs time and again:

> The stars peep behind her and peer;
> And I laugh to see them whirl and flee,
> Like a swarm of golden bees,
> When I widen the rent in my wind-built tent,
> Till the calm rivers, lakes, and seas,
> Like strips of the sky fallen through me on high,
> Are each paved with the moon and these.

The grotesque 'and these' is an affront to all prosaic discipline. So again:

> I am the daughter of Earth and Water,
> And the nursling of the Sky;
> I pass through the pores of the ocean and shores;
> I change but I cannot die . . .

—where 'ocean and shores' is unthinkable in speech or prose. And finally:

> From cape to cape, with a bridge-like shape,
>> Over a torrent sea,
> Sunbeam-proof, I hang like a roof,—
>> The mountains its columns be.

Here the language is quite indiscriminate; the adjectival 'torrent' is a Latinate urbanity, 'sunbeam-proof' is an audacious coining, and 'The mountains . . . be' is a *naïveté*.

Obviously the conduct of the metaphor in the second stanza is a more serious flaw than any of these later examples. And obviously too, Shelley pitches his poem in a high key, to advise us not to expect nicety of discrimination and prosaic sense. The poem offers compensations. But all the same when the barbarities are so brutal and the carelessness so consistent, it may be doubted whether we can let them pass on any understanding. In poems of this sort, the weight to be given to diction and invention respectively is something that must be left to the taste of the reader. But this may serve as an example of how, even in sublime poems, the poet may take such liberties with his diction as to estrange his reader's sympathies. For one reader, at any rate, "The Cloud" remains a poem splendid in conception but ruined by licentious phrasing.

(ii) *Shelley and the Familiar Style*

This does not dispose of Shelley's pretensions to sublimity. They confuse at almost every point the issue of his diction. In reading Wordsworth it is comparatively easy to distinguish the 'sublime' poems from the others, and to say that this poem begs the question of diction, this other does not. In the case of Shelley this is not so easily done. And yet there are poems by Shelley which plainly make no sublime pretensions. It was Ernest de Selincourt, I think, who proposed Shelley as one of the masters of the familiar style. The term, like all those which we find we need, is out of fashion; but plainly it refers to a quality of tone, of unflurried ease between poet and reader, in short to urbanity, the distinctive virtue of a pure diction.

It is worth remarking how unlikely this was, in the period when Shelley wrote. Plainly urbanity will come most easily to a poet who is sure of his audience, sure that he and his reader share a broad basis of conviction and assumption. The whole pressure of Shelley's age was against anything of the kind. Urbanity, except in the raffish version of Byron and Praed, was out of fashion among critics and readers; but that was the least of the difficulties. In the Elizabethan, the Caroline and the Augustan ages, the poet moved in a society more or less stable and more or less in agreement about social propriety. Most poets moved in circles where manners were ceremonious. The courteous usages were mostly hypocritical, but at least they were con-sistent; and they furnished the poet with a model urbanity which he could preserve in the tone of his writing. This was as true of the ponderous decorum of Mrs. Thrale's drawing-room as of the elaborate frivolity of the court of Charles II. Presumably, the violent dis-location of English society at the end of the eighteenth century (the Industrial Revolution) had destroyed the established codes of social behaviour. At any rate, in the Godwin household, in the family of Leigh Hunt, in the extraordinary domestic arrangements of Lord Byron, personal suffering and passion broke through into conversation and social demeanour. These were people who lived on their nerves, whom an established code of behaviour no longer protected. Therefore we cannot expect to find in the poetry of 1820 the exquisite assurance, the confident communication between poet and reader, which dignifies the slightest pieces of Thomas Carew or Thomas Parnell. We cannot expect it; but we find it. It is only natural that Spenser and Dryden, Carew and Parnell, enjoy this assurance. It is anything but natural, it seems almost impossible, that Shelley should do so.

The familiar style in this sense derives from the mean style of the Elizabethans, distinguished by them from the high style, proper to the heroic poem and the hymn, and from the base style of satire and pastoral. It is related too, to what Coleridge, in *Biographia Literaria*, called the 'neutral' style. It is distinguished from the other styles, in the nineteenth century as in the sixteenth, by being comparatively prosaic. Now, according to Johnson, a diction was pure when it was sanctioned by speech-usage on the one hand, and by literary precedent (classic and neo-classic) on the other. The poet's needs tugged him now one way, now the other; to tread a middle course, in touch with both sorts of usage, was to write a pure diction. But as the literary models varied (Juvenal for satire, Virgil for epic), so did the spoken models. The speech of a cobbler was not the model for epic, nor the speech of bishops for satire.

There survived, in fact, though mostly unacknowledged, Puttenham's rule that the model for the high style was the speech of courtiers and governors; for the mean style, the speech of merchants and yeomen; for the base style, the speech of peasants and menial trades. In theory Wordsworth ignored the other criterion, literary precedent, and, as Coleridge confusedly saw, came near to asserting that the only permissible style was the mean. In any of the styles, to maintain a pure diction was to preserve 'the tone of the centre' which Arnold was to esteem in Attic prose. It is one way of explaining 'the sublime', to say that, as England in the eighteenth century became a bourgeois state, the spoken model for the high style disappeared, and in poetry which 'affected the sublime' (the Augustan version of the high style) the question, whether the diction was pure, became meaningless. We are usually asked to acknowledge that Shelley's greatest poetry was of this sort. But there are other poems which are in the base and the mean styles; and it is among these that we have to look for Shelley the master of the familiar style.

The clearest example of Shelley's base style is the "Letter to Maria Gisborne". If we continue to talk in terms of Elizabethan decorum, this corresponds to "The Shepheard's Calender", as "Julian and Maddalo", in the mean style, to "Colin Clout's Come Home Again", as "The Cloud", in the high style, to "Fowre Hymnes". Shelley himself invites the Spenserian parallel:

> Near those a most inexplicable thing,
> With lead in the middle—I'm conjecturing

How to make Henry understand; but no—
I'll leave, as Spenser says, with many mo,
This secret in the pregnant womb of time,
Too vast a matter for so weak a rhyme.[1]

The archaism, like others ('I wist' . . . 'they swink')
is used partly as Spenser used it in "The Shepheards
Calender" or "Mother Hubberd's Tale", partly as
Byron used it in "Don Juan", to draw attention to its
ungainly self. But the "Letter to Maria Gisborne" is
neither Spenserian nor Byronic. It belongs to the tradition of Donne and Browning, who use the base style
to unusual ends. There is no gainsaying that Shelley's
verse resembles Browning's more than Donne's; it is
an exercise in agility, not energy. Still, it is heartening,
not hearty; and affectionate without being mawkish.
It is too exuberant to be called urbane in the usual
sense. But it is so, in the sense that the poet is sure of his
relationship with the person he addresses, that he knows
what is due to her and to himself, that he maintains a
consistent tone towards her. She is not a peg to hang a
poem on, nor a bosom for him to weep on, but a person
who shares with him certain interests and certain friends
and a certain sense of humour.

This poem is prosaic only in the relatively unimport-
ant sense that it introduces things like hackney-coaches,
Baron de Tott's Memoirs, 'self-impelling steam-
wheels', and 'a queer broken glass With ink in it'. But
like Donne's verse or Browning's, Shelley's is far more
figurative than normal prose. For truly lean and bare
prosaic language, we turn to "Julian and Maddalo":

[1] Or, as Sidney says (Astrophel and Stella):
      "Too high a theme for my low style to show".

I rode one evening with Count Maddalo
Upon the bank of land which breaks the flow
Of Adria towards Venice; a bare strand
Of hillocks, heaped from ever-shifting sand,
Matted with thistles and amphibious weeds,
Such as from earth's embrace the salt ooze breeds
Is this; an uninhabited sea-side,
Which the lone fisher, when his nets are dried,
Abandons; and no other object breaks
The waste, but one dwarf tree and some few stakes
Broken and unrepaired, and the tide makes
A narrow space of level sand thereon,
Where 'twas our wont to ride while day went down.

This of course represents a specifically Romantic purity —the adoption, from prose or careful conversation, of a vocabulary of natural description. At their best, the eighteenth-century poets had good reason for believing that features of natural appearance had to be dignified by figures, if they were to be pleasing and instructive; but more often their fussing with metaphors and personifications represented an impurity even by their own standards, for there can be little doubt that their practice in this particular was very far from any spoken usage. Shelley's assumption, that accuracy confers its own dignity, produced a much purer diction; and there are satisfying examples of this elsewhere in "Julian and Maddalo", as elsewhere in his work.[1] But what the Romantics gained with one hand they lost from the other. For if Johnson, for example, was 'intolerably poetical' when he essayed natural description, he had an enviable prosaic assurance in his dealings with the

---

[1] Notably in "Lines" (1815), "The Sunset" (1816), "Summer and Winter" (1820) and "Evening: Ponte al Mare, Pisa" (1821).

abstractions of moral philosophy. And it is in this province that Shelley's diction is woefully impure. He expressed, in *The Defence of Poetry*, his concern for these large abstractions, and his Platonic intention to make them apprehensible and 'living' in themselves. In 'The Witch of Atlas" he came near to effecting this; but more often, this programme only means that an abstraction such as Reason or Justice must always be tugged about in figurative language. The moment they appear in Shelley's verse (and they always come in droves) the tone becomes hectic, the syntax and punctuation disintegrate. In "Julian and Maddalo", by inventing the figure and the predicament of the maniac, Shelley excuses this incoherency and presents it (plausibly enough) as a verbatim report of the lunatic's ravings: and in this way he preserves the decorum of the conversation piece (the poem is sub-titled "A Conversation"). As a result, the whole of this passage, tiresome and unpoetic as it is, impairs but does not ruin the whole. The urbanity is resumed in the close:

> If I had been an unconnected man
> I, from this moment, should have formed some plan
> Never to leave sweet Venice,—for to me
> It was delight to ride by the lone sea;
> And then, the town is silent—one may write
> Or read in gondolas by day or night,
> Having the little brazen lamp alight,
> Unseen, uninterrupted; books are there,
> Pictures, and casts from all those statues fair
> Which were twin-born with poetry, and all
> We seek in towns, with little to recall
> Regrets for the green country. I might sit
> In Maddalo's great palace, and his wit

> And subtle talk would cheer the winter night
> And make me know myself, and the firelight
> Would flash upon our faces, till the day
> Might dawn and make me wonder at my stay.

The conversation we have attended to in the poem is just as civilized as the intercourse of Maddalo and Julian here described. It is in keeping that Julian should know little of Maddalo and not approve of all that he knows, but should be prepared to take him, with personal reservations, on his own terms. It is the habit of gentlemen; and the poet inculcates it in the reader, simply by taking it for granted in his manner of address. The poem civilizes the reader; that is its virtue and its value.

"To Jane; the Invitation" and "To Jane: the Recollection" were originally two halves of one poem, called "The Pine Forest of the Cascine near Pisa". In the second working over, "The Invitation" gained enormously, "The Recollection" hardly at all. The evolution of the latter poem illustrates very forcibly the process (analysed by Dr. Leavis) by which the characteristically Shelleyan attitude emerges from a Wordsworthian base. The original version is strikingly Wordsworthian in metre and diction:

> A spirit interfused around,
> > A thinking, silent life;
> To momentary peace it bound
> > Our mortal nature's strife;—
>
> And still, it seemed, the centre of
> > The magic circle there,
> Was one whose being filled with love
> > The breathless atmosphere.

This becomes:

> A spirit interfused around,
>   A thrilling, silent life,—
> To momentary peace it bound
>   Our mortal nature's strife;
> And still I felt the centre of
>   The magic circle there
> Was one fair form that filled with love
>   The lifeless atmosphere.

As Dr. Leavis notes, the changes ('thrilling' for 'thinking', 'being' to 'fair form', and 'lifeless' for 'breathless') are all in the direction of eroticism. It is more pertinent to the present enquiry to notice that they all remove the discourse further from prosaic sense. One could write, in sober prose, of a *'breathless'* atmosphere; one could never describe it as *'lifeless'*. And by the same token a prose-writer can make us conceive how a person can seem to imbue a locality or a moment with a peculiar spiritual flavour; but that the emanation should be physical, an attribute of 'form' rather than 'being', is something far more difficult. It is, of course, part of the poetic function to persuade us of realities outside the range of prosaic sense. But this can hardly be done by the familiar tone; and certainly Shelley does not do it here. He does not persuade us of the novelty, he only tricks us into it. His verse neither appeals to an old experience, nor creates a new one. These passages are a serious flaw in such a short poem.

The other piece, "The Invitation", is a nonpareil, and one of Shelley's greatest achievements. It maintains the familiar tone, though in highly figured language, and contrives to be urbane about feelings which are novel and remote. This poem presents the experience which "The Recollection" tries to define and rationalize; and the definition is there, already, in the expression. Jane's influence upon the scene where she moved is here entirely credible; what Shelley afterwards tried to express, first in Wordsworthian and then in erotic terms, here persuades us from the start with no fuss or embarrassment. It is the lack of fuss, the ease and assurance, which persuades us throughout. In other words, the poem is first and foremost a triumph of tone. We can accept Jane as 'Radiant Sister of the Day', largely because the lyrical feeling has already accommodated such seemingly unmanageable things as unpaid bills and unaccustomed visitors. It is an achievement of urbanity to move with such ease from financial and social entanglements to elated sympathy with a natural process; just as it is a mark of civilization to be able to hold these things together in one unflurried attitude.

(iii) *"The Sensitive Plant" and "The Witch of Atlas"*

It is important that we should understand the reservations we have to make about "The Recollection". We dislike Shelley's eroticism, in the end, because it seems a vicious attitude, morally reprehensible; but we dislike it in the first place only because it produces a vicious diction, a jargon. In the end every true literary judgment is a moral judgment. But many critics go wrong, and many readers misunderstand them, because they pass too rapidly into the role of moralist. Even so, those critics are doing their duty better than others who think that moral judgment is no part of their business.

I think we should value the significant ambiguity in such phrases as '*chaste* diction', '*pure* diction', '*vicious* style', 'the *conduct* of a fable'. But I am willing to let the ambiguity tell its own tale and to stop short, in this argument, before the point at which literary criticism moves over and becomes philosophical. It is best to think, therefore, that we condemn Shelley's eroticism (as we do) because it produces a jargon, and not because we dislike it 'in itself'.

For the Elizabethan, the love-song (the 'praise' or the 'complaint') demanded the mean style, unless it used the pastoral convention. And the best of Shelley's love-songs (not those, like "Love's Philosophy", which figure in the anthologies) are distinguished, like the best Caroline lyrics, by urbanity. As early as 1814, the "Stanza, written at Bracknell" can control self-pity by controlled and judicious phrasing:

> Thy dewy looks sink in my breast;
>   Thy gentle words stir poison there;
> Thou hast disturbed the only rest
>   That was the portion of despair!
> Subdued to Duty's hard control,
>   I could have borne my wayward lot:
> The chains that bind this ruined soul
>   Had cankered then—but crushed it not.

It is not serious, of course, only album-verse; as is some of Carew. It all depends on how good the album is; in other words, on the degree of civilization in the society which calls for such trifles. And of course there is no question of comparison with Carew. But the Caroline neatness in the third and fourth lines, and the Augustan echo in the fifth, represent an urbane control

which Shelley later threw away. More urbane still are
the stanzas, "To Harriet", written in the same year:

> Thy look of love has power to calm
> The stormiest passion of my soul;
> Thy gentle words are drops of balm
> In life's too bitter bowl;
> No grief is mine, but that alone
> These choicest blessings I have known.
>
> Harriet! if all who long to live
> In the warm sunshine of thine eye,
> That price beyond all pain must give,—
> Beneath thy scorn to die;
> Then hear thy chosen own too late
> His heart most worthy of thy hate.
>
> Be thou, then, one among mankind
> Whose heart is harder not for state,
> Thou only virtuous, gentle, kind,
> Amid a world of hate;
> And by a slight endurance seal
> A fellow-being's lasting weal.
>
> For pale with anguish is his cheek.
> His breath comes fast, his eyes are dim,
> Thy name is struggling ere he speak.
> Weak is each trembling limb;
> In mercy let him not endure
> The misery of a fatal cure.
>
> Oh trust for once no erring guide!
> Bid the remorseless feeling flee;
> 'Tis malice, 'tis revenge, 'tis pride
> 'Tis anything but thee;
> Oh, deign a nobler pride to prove,
> And pity if thou canst not love.

Of course we cheapen the idea of urbanity by applying

it to such polished nothings as these. But in their brittle elegance they represent a tradition which could have made Shelley's later love-verse a source of delight instead of embarrassment. The consciously elegant wording in places suggests another poet and even another period. Indeed there is more than a hint of pastiche; but that very period-flavour represents a discipline which Shelley threw away.

He can be seen doing so in the "Bridal Song" of 1821, which is admirable in its first version. In this first:

> O joy! O fear! what will be done
> In the absence of the sun!

—is as manly and wholesome as Suckling's "Ballad of a Wedding". In the last version:

> O joy! O fear! there is not one
> Of us can guess what may be done
> In the absence of the sun . . .

—is just not true. And the familiar tone of 'Come along!' which securely anchors the first version, is merely silly in the others.

As Dr. Leavis points out, it appears from parts of "Peter Bell the Third" that Shelley quite deliberately worked erotic elements into the Wordsworthian base of many of his poems. He seems to have mistaken for prudery the master's natural frigidity. No doubt, too, the erotic jargon was bound up with his dedicated flouting of all the sexual morality of his society. For whatever reason Shelley in his love-lyrics adopted a hectic and strident tone, and the urbanity of his early pieces never bore fruit. At the same time he threw into lyrical form more and more of his poetry. The lyric became confused with the hymn and so moved into the orbit of the sublime.

But the jargon came to be habitual with him, whatever sort of poem he wrote, until it taints them nearly all, sublime or not. One of the least tainted is "The Sensitive Plant", which I find one of his greatest achievements, and of great interest from the point of view of diction. In this poem and "The Witch of Atlas" Shelley is as daring as ever in invention, making his fable as wayward and arbitrary as possible. In both poems the sensuousness is of his peculiar sort which makes the familiar remote. (He takes a common object such as a rose or a boat, and the more he describes it, the less we remember what it is.) In short, the vision in both these poems has all the difficulties of the Shelleyan sublime, impalpable and aetherial. What distinguishes these poems, however, from such a similar (and maddening) piece as "Alastor", is the presence, at the end of each of them, of a tough hawser of sober sense which at once pulls the preceding poem into shape and (what amounts to the same thing) gives it as much prose meaning as it will bear.

"The Sensitive Plant" is in three parts, with a conclusion. The first part presents in ecstatic detail the garden in summer, and dwells with particular weight upon one plant in the garden, which appears endowed with almost human intelligence in so far as it seeks to express the love it feels and the beauty it aspires to. Devoid of bloom and scent, it is unable to do so. But this predicament is subordinate to the poet's more general purpose, which is, in Part I, to make the garden

seem like a dream. He does so with persuasive ease,
partly by metrical resourcefulness (the metres induce
a dream, not a pre-Raphaelite swoon), partly by deliberate confusion between the five senses, and partly
by exploiting the vaporous, atmospheric and luminous
features in the scene which he describes. Part II is short
and concerned with the presiding human deity of the
garden, a woman who is a sort of human counterpart
of the Sensitive Plant. Part III begins with the death
of the lady and describes how the garden, through
autumn and winter into the next spring, falls into un-
weeded ruin.

In the scheme of this fable there is plainly room for
an erotic element. The garden, for all its dream-like
quality, pulses with germinating energy; and this 'love'
is what the sensitive plant seeks to express:

> But none ever trembled and panted with bliss
> In the garden, the field, or the wilderness,
> Like a doe in the noontide with love's sweet want,
> As the companionless Sensitive Plant.

We know Shelley's eroticism is vicious only by the
vicious diction it produces. Therefore we can have no
complaints about the third line of this stanza, at the
same time as we condemn the first. There the trembling
and the panting and the bliss, coming thus together,
are Shelleyan jargon, reach-me-down words which
obviate the need for thinking and feeling precisely.
The vice in question is not lasciviousness but more
generally self-indulgence which betrays itself in lax
phrasing as in lax conduct. Once we have read a certain
amount of Shelley's verse, we recognize and dislike

words from the private jargon, even when they are used
with propriety:

> And the hyacinth purple, and white, and blue,
> Which flung from its bells a sweet peal anew
> Of music so delicate, soft, and intense,
> It was felt like an odour within the sense.

This is deliberate confusion between the senses, not
used as later poets used it for definition of a compound
sense-experience, nor only for intensification, but to
throw over waking experience the illusion of a dream.
Unfortunately 'intense' is a word we learn to suspect
in Shelley, and it irritates. So again:

> The plumed insects swift and free,
> Like golden boats on a sunny sea,
> Laden with light and odour, which pass
> Over the gleam of the living grass;

> The unseen clouds of the dew, which lie
> Like fire in the flowers till the sun rides high,
> Then wander like spirits among the spheres,
> Each cloud faint with the fragrance it bears;

> The quivering vapours of dim noontide,
> Which like a sea o'er the warm earth glide,
> In which every sound, and odour, and beam,
> Move as reeds in a single stream.

Here the confusion between the senses is particularly
persuasive, for it appeals to known facts about atmospheric conditions, or else to the evidence of the senses
in such conditions. Unfortunately 'faint' and 'dim' are
words from the jargon; and this perturbs the reader,
even though both are plausible in this context.

Occasionally, too, there are flagrant violations of
prosaic discipline:

But the Sensitive Plant which could give small fruit
Of the love which it felt from the leaf to the root,
Received more than all, it loved more than ever,
Where none wanted but it, could belong to the giver . . .

and:

The snowdrop, and then the violet,
Arose from the ground with warm rain wet,
And their breath was mixed with fresh odour, sent
From the turf like the voice and the instrument

—which is culpably ambiguous like Byron's lines which appalled Wordsworth:

I stood in Venice on the Bridge of Sighs
A palace and a prison on each hand.

And yet at the very crux of the argument lies the beautiful stanza:

And the beasts, and the birds, and the insects were drowned
In an ocean of dreams without a sound;
Whose waves never mark, though they ever impress
The light sand which paves it, consciousness.

This is memorably poetic, and yet, in the distinction between 'mark' and 'impress', and in the logical tautness of the whole image, it is 'strong' with the prosaic strength which Dr. Johnson found in Denham.

The object of these many examples is not to pick holes in a masterpiece, still less to reduce judgment to some ridiculous balancing of good stanzas against bad. They are meant to illustrate what is after all the capital difficulty in reading Shelley—his unevenness. He has hardly left one perfect poem, however short. In reading him one takes the good with the bad, or one does without it altogether. The business of private judgment on his poems is not a weighing of pros and cons but a decision whether the laxity, which is always there, lies at the centre of the poem (as it often does) or in the margin. I have no doubt that the faults of "The Sensitive Plant" are marginal, and that at the centre it is sound and strong.

In any case, the second and third parts of the poem are an improvement on Part I. Part III, in particular, presents a rank and desolate scene as in "Julian and Maddalo" but in greater detail. It is done more poetically than by Crabbe, but no less honestly.

The six stanzas of the "Conclusion" are of a quite different kind. They ask to be judged on the score of diction, and they triumphantly pass the test they ask for:

> Whether the Sensitive Plant, or that
> Which within its boughs like a Spirit sat,
> Ere its outward form had known decay,
> Now felt this change, I cannot say.
>
> Whether that Lady's gentle mind,
> No longer with the form combined
> Which scattered love, as stars do light,
> Found sadness, where it left delight,
>
> I dare not guess; but in this life
> Of error, ignorance, and strife,
> Where nothing is, but all things seem,
> And we the shadows of the dream,
>
> It is a modest creed, and yet
> Pleasant if one considers it,
> To own that death itself must be,
> Like all the rest, a mockery.

That garden sweet, that lady fair,
And all sweet shapes and odours there,
In truth have never passed away:
'Tis we, 'tis ours are changed; not they.

For love, and beauty, and delight,
There is no death nor change: their might
Exceeds our organs, which endure
No light, being themselves obscure.

There is not a phrase here which would be out of place in unaffected prose. If that is strange praise for a piece of poetry, it is what one can rarely say of the poetry of Shelley's period. If these stanzas stood by themselves, they might seem tame and flat. In their place in the longer poem they are just what is needed to vouch for the more florid language of what has gone before.

The only comparable achievement, among Shelley's poems, is "The Witch of Atlas". In most editions this poem is introduced by some loose-jointed jaunty stanzas in which Shelley replies to the objection that his poem is lacking in human interest. He compares it with "Peter Bell":

Wordsworth informs us he was nineteen years
        Considering and re-touching Peter Bell;
Watering his laurels with the killing tears
        Of slow, dull care, so that their roots to Hell
Might pierce, and their wide branches blot the spheres
        Of Heaven, with dewy leaves and flowers; this well
May be, for Heaven and Earth conspire to foil
The over-busy gardener's blundering toil.

My Witch indeed is not so sweet a creature
        As Ruth or Lucy, whom his graceful praise
Clothes for our grandsons—but she matches Peter,
        Though he took nineteen years, and she three days

In dressing. Light the vest of flowing metre
　　She wears; he, proud as dandy with his stays,
Has hung upon his wiry limbs a dress
Like King Lear's 'looped and windowed raggedness'.

If you strip Peter, you will see a fellow
　　Scorched by Hell's hyperequatorial climate
Into a kind of a sulphureous yellow:
　　A lean mark, hardly fit to fling a rhyme at;
In shape a Scaramouch, in hue Othello.
　　If you unveil my Witch, no priest nor primate
Can shrive you of that sin,—if sin there be
In love, when it becomes idolatry.

The point of the comparison with "Peter Bell" is not very clear. The implication is that both poems are free fantasies, and that Wordsworth spoiled his by labouring it, whereas the essential virtue of such pieces is their spontaneity, and this Shelley claims to achieve. More interesting is the question how far such poems will bear scrutiny for meanings, how far such fantasies can be treated as allegorical. This I take to be the question of the last stanza above, and Shelley's answer is rather ambiguous. He begins by warning the reader not to rationalize at all, implying that Wordsworth came to grief by inviting such a reading; but then, in the teasing play with 'love' and 'idolatry', he seems to allow that to look for an allegory is perhaps the best tribute one can give. At any rate, it seems plain that "The Witch of Atlas", like "Kubla Khan" no less than "Peter Bell", is a flight of gratuitous fancy, a sort of iridescent bubble in which the reader looks for a 'message' only at his peril.

And of course the poem is all that Shelley says—a wayward fable, set in an unearthly landscape peopled by creatures neither human nor divine. Like "Alastor" and "The Sensitive Plant" it has no meaning except as a whole. It is one half of a vast metaphor with the human term left out; and this, its meaning for human life, emerges from the shape of the whole or else it is lost for ever. It was lost in "Alastor", and to give the meaning in an Introduction (as Shelley did then) is not enough. The meaning may fit the myth, but it is not carried in the myth, and one always forgets what "Alastor" is about. "The Witch of Atlas", which is just as wayward and inhuman, takes on meaning, as much meaning as it can bear without cracking the singing voice. Shelley takes care of the meaning:

> The priests would write an explanation full,
> Translating hieroglyphics into Greek,
> How the God Apis really was a bull,
> And nothing more; and bid the herald stick
> The same against the temple doors, and pull
> The old cant down; they licensed all to speak
> Whate'er they thought of hawks, and cats, and geese,
> By pastoral letters to each diocese.

It is absurd, of course. We cannot really believe that the ideal beauty of the vision means no more in moral terms than the regeneration of religious institutions, and their purification from superstition. But Shelley admits the absurdity, by his verse-form, at the same time as he implies that such a change must after all be *part* of any regenerated world. There is no danger of taking this too seriously, and thereby damaging the sheer creative *élan* of the poem. And by thus slipping back, at the end of the poem, into the familiar, even slangy base style of the prefatory stanzas, Shelley guards this most visionary and fantastic poem from any rough handling. He casts his myth into a sort of rough-hewn cradle of coarse sense. The device is the same as that in "The Sensitive Plant", except that here Shelley uses the base, where there he used the mean style. To complain that the poem is 'obscure' or 'lacking in human interest' is now out of the question. If one does so, one has missed the point, and made not a mistake only but a social blunder. To that extent Shelley's is an achievement, once again, of urbanity.

*

The poet I have considered here is a poet of poise and good breeding. Shelley was the only English Romantic poet with the birth and breeding of a gentleman, and that cannot be irrelevant. What is more surprising is the evidence that in other poems Shelley failed chiefly for want of the very tact which is here conspicuous. I am at a loss to explain how a poet so well aware of what he was doing should also have written "The Cenci". But if urbanity depends on the relation between poet and public, then it may be that Shelley's failures in tact were connected with his being unread and neglected. In her notes on the poems of 1821, Mrs. Shelley hinted as much:

> Several of his slighter and unfinished poems were inspired by these scenes, and by the companions around us. It is the nature of that poetry, however, which overflows from the soul, oftener to express sorrow and regret than joy; for it is when oppressed by the weight of life, and away from those he loves, that the poet has recourse to the solace of expression in verse.

It is, alas, too true that many of Shelley's poems are the products of self-pity looking for 'solace' or compensation; and it is not strange that the 'slighter and un-finished poems', inspired by 'the companions around us', should be some of Shelley's best work. This is not the poetry 'which overflows from the soul', but the considered expression of an intelligent man.

IV

HOPKINS AS A DECADENT CRITIC

THERE are many ways of looking at the letters of Gerard Manley Hopkins. To the theologian and musician they can offer as much as to the critic and the prosodist. And anyone interested in the varieties of human friendship will find much to wonder at and admire. It is as a critic, however, that Hopkins is most surprising and most obviously impressive, for it is in his criticism that he is most plainly ahead of his time. His opinions of the verse of his contemporaries chime almost exactly with the views reached, fifty years after his death, by the best modern poets and critics. And this clairvoyance, added to the prestige of his poetry, has made him in certain circles almost above reproach. It will be the object of this essay to point out that while his criticism, especially of poetry, is so influential, it can be dangerous. But because, in other circles, Hopkins as a poet can still be rejected out of hand, it is in place to say at the start that the present writer holds him to be perhaps the greatest Victorian poet, and the best critic of his age after Matthew Arnold. While making these claims, it is only fair to remind the reader that the Victorian age produced little great poetry *in any case*; and also to assure him that if Hopkins is the first critic after Arnold, he may come a long way after.

There is nothing to show that Hopkins' criticism developed very much from first to last. There is no great difference, in substance or in quality, between his first pronouncements and his latest. It is none the less convenient to observe an order roughly chronological, if only because the earliest statement of critical principles is also the most comprehensive. It occurs in a letter to Alexander William Mowbray Baillie, written in 1864, when Hopkins was twenty.[1] In this letter Hopkins divides the language of verse into three kinds. The first is the language of inspiration:

> The word inspiration need cause no difficulty. I mean by it a mood of great, abnormal in fact, mental acuteness, either energetic or receptive, according as the thoughts which arise in it seem generated by a stress or action of the brain, or to strike into it unasked.

The second kind of language is Parnassian:

> It can only be spoken by poets, but is not in the highest sense poetry. It does not require the mood of mind in which the poetry of inspiration is written. It is spoken *on and from the level* of a poet's mind, not, as in the other case, when the inspiration which is the gift of genius, raises him above himself.

Parnassian is above all distinctive:

> Great men, poets I mean, have each their own dialect as it were of Parnassian, formed generally as they go on writing, and at last,—this is the point to be marked,—they can see things in this Parnassian way and describe them in this Parnassian tongue, without further effort of inspiration. In a poet's particular kind of Parnassian lies most of his style, of his manner, of his mannerism if you like.

The third kind of language is treated only in passing:

> The third kind is merely the language of verse as distinct from that of prose, Delphic, the tongue of the Sacred *Plain*, I may call it, used in common by poet and poetaster. Poetry when

[1] *Further Letters of Gerard Manley Hopkins*, ed. Abbott, pp. 69-73.

spoken is spoken in it, but to speak it is not necessarily to speak poetry.

There are also, he explains, two sub-kinds, the first Castalian, the second Olympian. Castalian is 'a higher sort of Parnassian', differing from the language of inspiration only because it lacks impersonality, is too characteristic of the writer. As for Olympian, "This is the language of strange masculine genius which suddenly, as it were, forces its way into the domain of poetry, without naturally having a right there. Milman's poetry is of this kind I think, and Rossetti's *Blessed Damozel*. But unusual poetry has a tendency to seem so at first."

It is remarkable how well these principles correspond with those in vogue to-day among the reviewers. For them 'Delphic' becomes 'poetic diction' (in a derogatory sense); 'Parnassian' is 'a distinctive voice', taken to be an improvement on the first stage; and 'the language of inspiration' is 'the profound impersonality of all art that is truly great'. The course of poetic advancement is often taken in this way to be from the impersonal (= 'undistinguished'), through the personal (= 'distinctive'), to the impersonal (= 'a disembodied voice'). But is it not true that the course may be run, without deviating into the personal? that the voice can move from 'undistinguished' to 'distinguished', without once being 'distinctive'? It may seem that in periods when 'poetic diction' was not in such bad odour as it was for Hopkins and is for us, when, in particular, it was accompanied by the idea of 'purity' ('a pure diction'), this possibility was recognized. It is worth while asking whether, if we follow

Hopkins in this (as I think we mostly do), we are limiting ourselves to a Victorian view of poetry, or whether we are only acceding to the extinction of a principle which was once fruitful but can be so no longer.

On joining the Society of Jesus, Hopkins destroyed the poetry he had written before 1868, and produced no more for about nine years. As might be expected, his letters in this period contain no criticism. With the re-awakening of his creative talent in 1877, criticism engages him again.

In 1878 appeared another guiding principle in Hopkins' criticism, his devotion to Milton:

> The same M. Arnold says Milton and Campbell are our two greatest masters of *style*. Milton's art is incomparable, not only in English literature, but, I should think, almost in any; equal, if not more than equal, to the finest of Greek or Roman. And considering that this is shewn especially in his verse, his rhythm and metrical system, it is amazing that so great a writer as Newman should have fallen into the blunder of comparing the first chorus of the *Agonistes* with the opening of *Thalaba* as instancing the gain in smoothness and correctness of versification made since Milton's time. . . .[1]

Milton is, for Hopkins, always the final court of appeal. And it is worth remarking that those modern readers who have most readily embraced Hopkins' poetry and his criticism are very often those who have called in question Milton's prestige, or at any rate the fruitfulness of his influence. Hopkins is quite unambiguous. He puts forward Milton, time and again, as a model; and in so doing he flies in the face not only of modern

[1] *The Correspondence of Gerard Manley Hopkins and Richard Watson Dixon*, ed. Abbott, p. 13.

poets, Ezra Pound and T. S. Eliot, but also of Keats and Cowper. In effect, he challenges one of the best authenticated working principles in the English poetic tradition—the principle that Milton, however great in himself, is a bad example for other poets. Was Hopkins alive to certain Miltonic aspects of his own poetry which his modern critics conspire to ignore, or merely cannot see? Of course he was indebted to Milton for the first hints of his novel prosody, and this is certainly one aspect of his art which has not engaged his later readers so much as he expected. But this does not entirely explain the matter; for Milton repeatedly appears in connection with 'Style' and, while this term is never fully explained by Hopkins, it plainly involves for him much more than prosody. It is quite possible of course that the critics may have seen the nature of Hopkins' achievement more clearly than he saw it himself; and that where he thought himself indebted to Milton, he was mistaken. But for students of his criticism the problem remains. Milton's practice is central to that criticism; and this must make it very different from the criticism of Keats, of Cowper or of Mr. Eliot. It is worth asking where and how Hopkins differs from these authorities, and whether he differs for the better or for the worse.

'Miltonic style' soon appears in connection with another important principle, as novel as that of 'Parnassian', the idea of 'inscape':

No doubt my poetry errs on the side of oddness. I hope in time to have a more balanced and Miltonic style. But as air, melody, is what strikes me most of all in music and design in painting, so design, pattern or what I am in the habit of calling 'inscape' is what I above all aim at in poetry. Now it is the virtue of design, pattern, or inscape to be distinctive and it is the vice of distinctiveness to become queer. This vice I cannot have escaped.[1]

It has been found by critics of Hopkins' poetry that to explain 'inscape' it is necessary to explore the poet's theology and philosophy, especially his admiring study of Duns Scotus. The same, of course, is true of his criticism. Every system of criticism rests, explicitly or not, upon a moral philosophy, and to do justice to the criticism one should ideally set it in that context. On the other hand I am concerned with how far Hopkins' standards of criticism are viable, how far they can be adopted with profit by readers professing quite different philosophies. And for this purpose it is enough to point out that, for Hopkins, since "it is the virtue of design, pattern, or inscape to be distinctive", this principle is closely related to 'the Parnassian'. Hopkins shows himself here aware of some of the dangers inherent in giving to 'distinctiveness' such value as he does. It is interesting to know how he intended to guard against those dangers, or whether he thought them only a risk that must be run.

To 1870 belong most of the snap-judgments that show Hopkins at his best. There is the comment on Swinburne, for instance:

I do not think that kind goes far: it expresses passion but not feeling, much less character. This I say in general or of Swinburne in particular. Swinburne's genius is astonishing, but it will, I think, only do one thing.[2]

[1] *The Letters of Gerard Manley Hopkins to Robert Bridges*, ed. Abbott, p. 66.
[2] *Letters to Bridges*, p. 79.

Or this on Tennyson:

> . . . there may be genius uninformed by character. I sometimes
> wonder at this in a man like Tennyson: his gift of utterance is truly
> golden, but go further home and you come to thoughts common-
> place and wanting in nobility (it seems hard to say it but I think
> you know what I mean). In Burns there is generally recognized
> a richness and beauty of manly character which lends worth to
> some of his smallest fragments, but there is a great want in his
> utterance; it is never really beautiful, he had no eye for pure
> beauty, he gets no nearer than the fresh picturesque expressed in
> fervent and flowing language. . . .[1]

Or the comment on the age:

> For it seems to me that the poetical language of an age should
> be the current language heightened, to any degree heightened
> and unlike itself, but not (I mean normally: passing freaks and
> graces are another thing) an obsolete one. That is Shakespeare's
> and Milton's practice and the want of it will be fatal to Tenny-
> son's Idylls and plays, to Swinburne, and perhaps to Morris.[2]

Or, more generally, on obscurity:

> One of two kinds of clearness one should have—either the
> meaning to be felt without effort as fast as one reads or else, if
> dark at first reading, when once made out *to explode*.[3]

This certainly does not exhaust the question of how a
poet transmits his meanings, but it could hardly be
bettered as a handy rule-of-thumb. In the same way,
many readers will admire the way the critic goes at once
to the heart of the matter, in the judgments on his contemporaries. But even here there are puzzling elements.
However warmly we may agree that "the poetical
language of an age should be the current language

---

[1] *Letters to Bridges*, p. 95.   [2] *Ibid.* p. 89.   [3] *Ibid.* p. 90.

heightened", we are not used to seeing Milton cited as an authority for it. Keats, we remember, discarded the Miltonic "Hyperion" just because 'English must be kept up'. And in the same way, we may be sure that Hopkins is right about Tennyson and yet wonder if he is right about Burns. "He had no eye for pure beauty . . ."—we suspect that 'pure beauty' never meant anything exact, and we should blush to see it in critical parlance to-day. Whatever the force of 'pure', we may find it a narrow notion of beauty that cannot find room for 'the fresh picturesque'. And does not such a narrowness reflect upon the critic?

The evidence of Hopkins' own poetry and what we know of his age can help us without much trouble to understand 'inscape' on the one hand, and 'pure beauty' on the other, whatever we may think of their value as critical terms. And his own account of 'Parnassian' and the related categories is sufficiently clear. What gives most trouble is his usage of 'Style'. It recurs in his detailed criticism of poems by Bridges:

And 'pleasurable' is a prosaic word, I think: can you not find something better? It is not a bad word, but it falls flatly. (This reminds me that 'test' is to my ear prosaic in 'Thou didst delight', but could scarcely be changed.) Otherwise the poem is very beautiful, very fine in execution and style. Style seems your great excellence, it is really classical. What fun if you were a classic! So few people have style, except individual style or manner—not Tennyson nor Swinburne nor Morris, not to name the scarecrow misbegotten Browning crew. Just think of the blank verse these people have exuded, such as *Paracelsus*, *Aurora Leigh*, Baillie's or Bayley's *Festus*, and so on. The Brownings are very fine too in their ghastly way.[1]

[1] *Letters to Bridges*, p. 111.

This is very puzzling. 'Style', thus called 'classical' and opposed to 'manner', might seem to approach the Augustan notion of 'a pure diction'. Hopkins applauds both Dixon and Bridges for the beauty of gentlemanly character in all they write, and this might have something to do with a sort of serious urbanity which we can readily associate with such a diction. Moreover, Hopkins is a stickler for propriety, as when he takes Bridges to task for confusing 'disillusion' and 'disenchantment'.[1] But we have already seen that, for Hopkins, 'classical' means 'Miltonic'. And what is more, the compliment is surely a left-handed one, since we have already learnt that what Hopkins values most in poetry is 'inscape', the distinctive. In denying to Bridges 'individual style or manner', Hopkins seems to deny him 'inscape', and plainly the language of Bridges can be neither Castalian nor Parnassian, since these are pre-eminently distinctive. It must be either 'Delphic' or else 'the language of inspiration', and since the complimentary intention is clear, it must be the latter. And indeed since he tries always for 'inscape', and 'inscape' is distinctive, it seems as if in his own poetry Hopkins commits himself to just that Parnassian which elsewhere he relegates to a second rank. This is in effect a *reductio ad absurdum*.

The point becomes a little clearer in a letter to Dixon of 1881, which is the fullest review by Hopkins of the English poetry of his own century:

The Lake poets and all that school represent, as it seems to me, the mean or standard of English style and diction, which

[1] *Letters to Bridges*, p. 121.

culminated in Milton but was never very continuous or vigor-
ously transmitted, and in fact none of these men unless perhaps
Landor were great masters of style, though their diction is
generally pure, lucid, and unarchaic.[1]

It is now clear that when Hopkins discerns 'Style', he
discerns Miltonic style. It is important that the language
of poets should be current and should observe propriety without being prosaic, and most of his contemporaries he thinks fail to observe these rules, but to
observe them is not to guarantee 'Style'. What is still
wanting appears to be some sort of consistent elevation.
If the language has all these, then it may be Miltonic
and will therefore be 'Style'. The chief difficulty which
remains is Hopkins' assumption that the language of
Milton is somehow 'current'; and some readers may
find this hard to concede.

As 'Style' is one of Milton's virtues, 'inscape' is the
other. Now since 'inscape' is distinctive and admirable,
and 'Parnassian' is distinctive and regrettable, and
since it is absurd to suppose that Hopkins set out to
write Parnassian, it follows that 'inscape' has little or
nothing to do with language at all, but is a quality of
form and design. The poet who seeks 'inscape' (Hopkins himself) must make his language current, proper
and clear, and he may even, by adding elevation, attain
to 'Style'. (Hopkins, as we have seen, hoped to achieve
'a more balanced and Miltonic style', though he knew
his other aim, distinctiveness, made it difficult.) But he
has a task above or apart from this, a matter of distinctive
formal disposition or moulding.

This notion engages Hopkins more and more:

---

[1] *Correspondence with Dixon*, p. 98.

In general I take it that other things being alike unity of action is higher the more complex the plot; it is the more difficult to effect and therefore the more valuable when effected. We judge so of everything.[1]

But how could you think such a thing of me as that I should in cold blood write 'fragments of a dramatic poem'?—I of all men in the world. To me a completed fragment, above all of a play, is the same unreality as a prepared impromptu.[2]

Now this is the artist's most essential quality, masterly execution: it is a kind of male gift and especially marks off men from women, the begetting one's thought on paper, on verse, on whatever the matter is; the life must be conveyed into the work and be displayed there, not suggested as having been in the artist's mind: otherwise the product is one of those hen's-eggs that are good to eat and look just like live ones but never hatch.[3]

It would be easy and idle to relate the metaphors of this last to 'Time's eunuch' (which occurs in the letters as well as the poem) and to the celibate rule. This train of thought may have had a special significance for the poet. For us, the three passages quoted point in the direction of something lost to English poetry since the Renaissance. We come nearest to what Hopkins meant by 'execution' by recalling Sidney's "Apologie for Poetry" or an expression of Gabriel Harvey's—'excellentest artificiality'. What is meant by 'execution' and 'inscape' is the Renaissance idea of poem as artifact, a shape in space and time, added to creation, thrown out by will and energy, and the more elaborate the better. But if the artifact reappears, it is only with a difference. Sidney's poem was something added to the world, cut

---

[1] *Correspondence with Dixon*, p. 113.
[2] *Letters to Bridges*, p. 218.
[3] *Correspondence with Dixon*, p. 133.

loose of its maker, absolute, anonymous, in its own right. The maker's energy was all to the casting forth, the endowment of independent life, the cutting of the threads from maker to made thing. Hopkins' poem on the contrary is to be distinctive; the systematic elaboration, and the setting of self-imposed tasks, generate the energy which throws the poem away from the poet, but only to the end that the reader, admiring the elaborate self-sufficiency, shall infer the energy and the shape of the making mind, and so work back to the poet again. The poet attempts a brilliant finesse. Things turn inside out. If he attains to 'Style', his impersonality is so conspicuous that it becomes his most intriguing personal trait; if he attains to 'inscape', the artificiality, the lack of intimacy, is the most intimate thing in the poem.

Such self-regarding ingenuity may be called decadent. Hopkins wrote in a decadent age, and if he is its greatest poet, he may be so because he cultivates his hysteria and pushes his sickness to the limit. Certainly he displays, along with the frantic ingenuity, another decadent symptom more easily recognized, the refinement and manipulation of sensuous appetite. This is an important, perhaps the essential, part of that pure beauty which he recognized in Tennyson and missed in Burns, a quality of hectic intensity. Much of his work, in criticism and poetry alike, is concerned with restoring to a jaded palate the capacity for enjoyment. There is an interesting letter to Dixon, very revealing in this connection:

I remember that crimson and pure blues seemed to me spiritual and heavenly sights fit to draw tears once; now I can just see what I once saw, but can hardly dwell on it and should not care to do so.[1]

And, in his latest letters, there is a mild controversy with Patmore about Keats:

> Since I last wrote I have reread Keats a little and the force of your criticism on him has struck me more than it did. It is impossible not to feel with weariness how his verse is at every turn abandoning itself to an unmanly and enervating luxury. It appears too that he said something like 'O for a life of impressions instead of thoughts'. It was, I suppose, the life he tried to lead. The impressions are not likely to have been all innocent and they soon ceased in death. His contemporaries, as Wordsworth, Byron, Shelley, and even Leigh Hunt, right or wrong, still concerned themselves with great causes, as liberty and religion; but he lived in mythology and fairyland the life of a dreamer. Nevertheless I feel and see in him the beginnings of something opposite to this, of an interest in higher things and of powerful and active thought.[2]

Hopkins, it may be thought, misses the point, which is not that some of Keats' experiences cannot have been innocent, but that the whole of Keats' programme may have been 'vicious'. In his most important poems, the Odes, this is the question which Keats explores.

Of course, it is plain why Hopkins could not agree with Patmore about Keats. His earliest work, the school prize-poems, are conspicuously Keatsian, and revel in an excess of sensuous luxury; and of course this luxury is a conspicuous feature of all his verse. It is possible that Hopkins thought to counterbalance this Keatsian effeminacy by the strenuous masculinity of 'inscape'; perhaps for some readers he does so and thereby attains

[1] *Correspondence with Dixon*, p. 38.
[2] *Further Letters*, pp. 237, 238.

a human mean, not decadent at all. Others again may find the compensating masculinity not in 'inscape' at all but in the taut frame of intellectual argument in all the poems, an important aspect of his poetry which the poet seems to take curiously for granted. (One may suspect that it was this, more than rhythm or diction which baffled Bridges sometimes; if so, neither Bridges nor Hopkins realized it.) Other readers again may find that 'inscape' and sensuous luxury go together and make the poetry decadent, and that the strict Jesuitical logic, for all its discipline, is not really a sign of health, but only another aspect of that systematizing elaboration which produced the doctrine of 'inscape' and the prosody. One has to leave this margin for difference of opinion, for if 'decadent' occurs in the critic's vocabulary at all, it comes at the point where criticism is not distinguishable from moral philosophy.

At any rate, one cannot read the letters, even where they are concerned with music or the classical studies in the Dorian rhythms, without feeling that the systematic and the elaborate have a value for Hopkins in themselves, and not merely as instruments for reaching after truth. The doctrine of 'inscape' admits as much. His thinking is casuistical. The most remarkable example of the value of the systematic for Hopkins is his letter to Bridges about Whitman:

Extremes meet, and (I must for truth's sake say what sounds pride) this savagery of his art, this rhythm in its last ruggedness and decomposition into common prose, comes near the last elaboration of mine. For that piece of mine is very highly wrought. The long lines are not rhythm run to seed: everything is weighed and timed in them. Wait till they have taken hold of your ear and you will find it so. No, but what it *is* like is the rhythm of Greek tragic choruses or of Pindar: which is pure sprung rhythm. And that has the same changes of cadence from point to point as this piece. If you want to try it, read one till you have settled the true places of the stress, mark these, then read it aloud, and you will see. Without this these choruses are prose bewitched; with it they are sprung rhythm like that piece of mine.[1]

The upshot of this is that Hopkins does not use his special rhythms in order to catch the movement of living speech. That is Whitman's policy but it is only Hopkins' starting-point. His rhythms differ from Whitman's (and by implication they are superior to Whitman's) sheerly because they are reduced to or elaborated into a system. Hopkins is systematic where Whitman is casual. And there, in the systematizing, resides the distinctive, the masculine, the 'inscape'.

Surely something the same is true of Hopkins' language. We applaud him, and rightly, for making his language current and refusing archaism. But again that is only the start; the language is anything but current by the time Hopkins has finished with it. And of course that was his doctrine; poetic language must be based on the current speech but it could be elevated and elaborated *ad lib.*, as, in his view, it was by Milton. He says of Dryden:

I can scarcely think of you not admiring Dryden without, I may say, exasperation. And my style tends always more towards Dryden. What is there in Dryden? Much, but above all this: he is the most masculine of our poets; his style and his rhythms lay the strongest stress of all our literature on the naked thew and

[1] *Letters to Bridges*, p. 157.

sinew of the English language, the praise that with certain qualifications one would give in Greek to Demosthenes, to be the greatest master of bare Greek.[1]

And what he says of Dryden has been applied by admiring critics to his own poems. But it does not really apply, or only with a difference. 'The naked thew and sinew' is not enough for Hopkins. It has to be crammed, stimulated and knotted together. He has no respect for the language, but gives it Sandow-exercises until it is a muscle-bound monstrosity. It is the Keatsian luxury carried one stage further, luxuriating in the kinetic and muscular as well as the sensuous. Word is piled on word, and stress on stress, to crush the odours and dispense a more exquisite tang, more exquisite than the life. To have no respect for language is to have none for life; both life and language have to be heightened and intensified, before Hopkins can approve them. He has been praised more warmly still; and it is contended that his use of language is Shakespearean. Certainly Shakespeare shows similar audacity. But the cases are not parallel. For Shakespeare there was not, in this sense, a language to respect. It was still in the melting-pot, fluid, experimental and expanding rapidly. Even in their speaking, Shakespeare's contemporaries were at liberty to coin, convert, transpose and cram together. Hopkins, like Doughty, treats nineteenth-century English as if it were still unstable and immature.

I think this is a true description of Hopkins' poetry, but to prove it one would need to move from point to point through several poems. At least such a view of language, poetic function, and human experience is

[1] *Letters to Bridges*, pp. 267, 268.

implied in the system of criticism. That system (and, though it is available in fragmentary form, it is truly systematic), however it may touch at several points upon modern criticism, is violently at odds with what distinguished later poets have laid down in theory or implied in critical practice. The gulf between Hopkins and Mr. Pound, for instance, or Mr. Eliot, is very wide, and can be shown most neatly perhaps by comparing the attitudes taken by the three poets towards Dante. For both Eliot and Pound, Dante has been consistently a pole of reference, in Mr. Eliot's specially limited sense 'a classic', and for both poets he has been in particular a model of poetic diction:

The border-line between 'gee whizz' and Milton's tumified dialect must exist (Dante in *De Vulgari Eloquio* seems to have thought of a good many particulars of the problem).[1]

The language of each great English poet is his own language; the language of Dante is the perfection of a common language.[2]

Hopkins' solitary comment on Dante is perhaps the most astonishing judgment in all three volumes of the letters:

This leads me to say that a kind of touchstone of the highest or most living art is seriousness; not gravity but the being in earnest with your subject—reality. It seems to me that some of the greatest and most famous works are not taken in earnest enough, are farce (where you ask the spectator to grant you something not only conventional but monstrous). I have this feeling about *Faust* and even about the *Divine Comedy*, whereas *Paradise Lost* is most seriously taken. It is the weakness of the whole Roman literature.[3]

[1] *Letters of Ezra Pound*, ed. Paige, p. 349.
[2] T. S. Eliot, "Dante", in *Selected Essays*, p. 252.
[3] *Letters to Bridges*, p. 225.

It is true that Hopkins' judgment does not turn upon Dantesque diction, but seems rather related to the doctrinal differences between Scotist and Thomist. Nevertheless the judgment, from a Jesuit poet, is remarkable. And of course it is plain that there is, in Hopkins' criticism, no room for such a notion as 'the perfection of a common language' or for highly rating a language which strikes a mean between current slang and Miltonic elevation. When Hopkins writes of a mean style he means the Miltonic style, and when he writes of 'pure diction' he means no more than observation of propriety. When he esteems gentlemanliness or 'character' in the writing of Bridges and Dixon he means neither Arnold's urbanity nor the Aristotelean mean, but 'character' in the sense of 'a man of character', i.e. something built up and maintained by the will. Even 'the language of the poetic plain', we remember, is called 'Delphic', that is, vatic, esoteric and elevated.

It is true, of course, that not only Hopkins but all the critics of his period were far from esteeming or even recognizing 'pure diction' in this sense. But Hopkins is further from it even than his contemporaries. The last passage quoted, for instance, makes play with what is obviously Hopkins' version of the 'high seriousness' of Arnold; and this may serve to remind us that in Hopkins' lifetime Arnold was the critic who came nearest to the idea of 'the perfection of a common language'. Arnold made the idea a principle in the criticism of prose, excluding it from poetry. His most elaborate statement of this position occurs in "The Literary Influence of Academies", where he finds that Attic prose is valuable because it maintains a valuable

urbanity, the tone and spirit of the centre as opposed
to the provincial spirit. He finds that there is a strong
tradition of such prose-writing in France, but he seeks
it in vain in England, where the masters of prose-style
(Jeremy Taylor, Burke, Ruskin, Kinglake) employ a
rhetorical 'poetic' prose. English prose comes nearest
to the Attic model in Addison or (in the critic's own
day) Newman. Hopkins valued Arnold's criticism and
rebuked Bridges for calling him 'Mr. Kid-glove Cock-
sure'. He mentions "The Literary Influence of
Academies" in a letter of 1864 to Baillie:

> You must also read, if you have not done so, Matthew Arnold
> on "The literary influence of Academies" in the August *Corn-
> hill*. Much that he says is worth attention, but, as is so often the
> case, in censuring bad taste he falls into two flagrant pieces of
> bad taste himself. I am coming to think much of taste myself,
> good taste and moderation, I who have sinned against them so
> much. But there is a prestige about them which is indescribable.[1]

It is more than twenty years later that he gives what is
obviously his considered rejoinder to Arnold's argument. It occurs in a letter to Patmore:

> . . . when I read your prose and when I read Newman's and
> some other modern writers' the same impression is borne in on
> me: no matter how beautiful the thought, nor, taken singly, with
> what happiness expressed, you do not know what *writing prose* is.
> At bottom what you do and what Cardinal Newman does is to
> think aloud, to think with pen to paper. In this process there are
> certain advantages; they may outweigh those of a perfect technic;
> but at any rate they exclude that; they exclude the belonging
> technic, the belonging rhetoric, the own proper eloquence of
> written prose. Each thought is told off singly and there follows a

[1] *Further Letters*, p. 74.

pause and this breaks the continuity, the *contentio*, the strain of address, which writing should usually have.

The beauty, the eloquence, of good prose cannot come wholly from the thought. With Burke it does and varies with the thought; when therefore the thought is sublime so does the style appear to be. But in fact Burke had no style properly so called: his style was colourlessly to transmit his thought. Still he was an orator in form and followed the common oratorical tradition, so that his writing has the strain of address I speak of above.

But Newman does not follow the common tradition—of writing. His tradition is that of cultured, the most highly educated, conversation; it is the flower of the best Oxford life. Perhaps this gives it a charm of unaffected and personal sincerity that nothing else could. Still he shirks the technic of written prose and shuns the tradition of written English. He seems to be thinking "Gibbon is the last great master of traditional English prose; he is its perfection: I do not propose to emulate him; I begin all over again from the language of conversation, of common life".

You too seem to me to be saying to yourself "I am writing prose, not poetry; it is bad taste and a confusion of kinds to employ the style of poetry in prose: the style of prose is to shun the style of poetry and to express one's views with point". But the style of prose is a positive thing and not the absence of verse-forms and pointedly expressed thoughts are single hits and give no continuity of style.[1]

Plainly Hopkins now so highly values 'inscape', elevation and distinctiveness that they are to be a principle of prose no less than poetry. The comments on Burke are quite unambiguous; Hopkins censures him because, when his thoughts were not sublime, neither was his style. This is as far as may be from what is almost taken for granted to-day, the principle that in any sort of

[1] *Further Letters*, pp. 231, 232.

writing that style is best which transmits most accurately the thought or the feeling of the writer.

As might be expected, Hopkins' judgments of his contemporaries are in general less acceptable to modern opinion when he speaks of prose-writers, than when he judges the poets. Stevenson is his hero:

In my judgment the amount of gift and genius which goes into novels in the English literature of this generation is perhaps not much inferior to what made the Elizabethan drama, and unhappily it is in great part wasted. How admirable are Blackmore and Hardy! Their merits are much eclipsed by the overdone reputation of the Evans-Eliot-Lewis-Cross woman (poor creature! one ought not to speak slightingly, I know), half real power, half imposition. Do you know the bonfire scenes in the *Return of the Native* and still better the sword-exercise scene in the *Madding Crowd*, breathing epic? or the wife-sale in the *Mayor of Casterbridge* (read by chance)? But these writers only rise to their great strokes; they do not write continuously well; now Stevenson is master of a consummate style and each phrase is finished as in poetry.[1]

The condescension to George Eliot of course has probably more to do with her sexual conduct than with her writing. Stevenson's 'consummate style' is chiefly a matter of 'word-painting'.[2] This narrow idea of the functions of prose-style corresponds to the narrowness of that 'pure beauty' which excluded Burns.

In 1886 'inscape' is still the ultimate criterion. The lack of it is damning to Sir Samuel Ferguson, for instance:

. . . for he was a poet; the *Forging of the Anchor* is, I believe, his most famous poem; he was a poet as the Irish are—to judge

[1] *Letters to Bridges*, pp. 238, 239.   [2] *Ibid*. p. 267.

by the little of his I have seen—full of feeling, high thoughts, flow of verse, point, often fine imagery and other virtues, but the essential and only lasting thing left out—what I call *inscape*, that is species or individually-distinctive beauty of style. . . .[1]

Plainly 'inscape' is the clue to whatever is still puzzling in Hopkins. And it is not necessary to examine its philosophical basis in his thought or its manifestation in his poems. It is time to ask what it means in simple terms of human personality. 'Inscape' is, we remember, specifically a Miltonic virtue. Now on Milton the man as distinct from the poet, there is only one comment among all the letters. It was made in 1877 to Bridges:

> Don't like what you say of Milton, I think he was a very bad man: those who contrary to our Lord's command both break themselves and, as St. Paul says, consent to those who break the sacred bond of marriage, like Luther and Milton, fall with eyes open into the terrible judgment of God.[2]

It does me little credit, perhaps, that I find here an anti-climax little short of comical. Of course 'the sacred bond of marriage' is an important matter. And I can well understand anyone, especially a Roman Catholic, who finds Milton 'a very bad man'; but I do not expect to find him called a bad man, only in the sense that George Eliot is 'a bad woman'. I expect to find the verdict go against Milton on more general and comprehensive grounds, precisely as a type of the extreme Protestant. One thinks to find the characteristic formulae of later Catholic writers—'individualism', perhaps, or 'humanistic arrogance', all that aspect of Milton which has to do with his ambivalent treatment of the Lucifer

---

[1] *Further Letters*, p. 225. [2] *Letters to Bridges*, p. 39.

figure. This is conspicuous by its absence from all Hopkins' comments on Milton. And it is not hard to see why. Hopkins' theory and his practice point in one direction. Put together such recurrent terms as 'inscape', 'sublime', 'distinctiveness', 'masculinity', 'character', and one is forced to the conclusion that it was just this, Milton's egotism, individualism and arrogance, which made him, for Hopkins, the model poet. His own poetry and his own criticism proceed from the single assumption that the function of poetry is to express a human individuality in its most wilfully uncompromising and provocative form. His is the poetry and the criticism of the egotistical sublime. Dixon answered the contention, that poetry was incompatible with membership of the Society of Jesus, by saying he could not see how one vocation could clash with the other. It was true, so long as the poet's vocation was conceived as Dixon conceived of it. But Hopkins knew better, and he was right too. He conceived of poetry as self-expression at its most relentless, as a vehicle for the individual will to impose itself on time. Between that and any sort of Christian calling there could be no compromise at all.

V

LANDOR'S SHORTER POEMS

To C. H. Herford, in 1897, it seemed that "Landor was . . . on the whole the greatest prose-writer of the age of Wordsworth; and, after Wordsworth, Coleridge, Byron, Shelley, and Keats, he was its greatest poet".[1] Whatever may be thought of Landor's prose, it would be hard to find anyone to-day to endorse the claim that, as a poet, he was greater than Scott, Clare, Crabbe, Hogg or Darley—all poets with whom Herford deals. I find him inferior to every one of these poets; but my intention here is not to gird at Herford or to sneer at Landor. For the latter has an importance out of proportion with his meagre achievement. At a crucial stage in the English poetic tradition he struck out alone a path of interesting and sensible experiment; and in deciding what chance there was of success, and where and how the experiment failed, we touch upon matters of importance for the writing of poetry at any time.

What Landor stood for in the writing of poetry can be seen from one of his more distinguished poems, "To Wordsworth":

> He who would build his fame up high,
> The rule and plummet must apply,
> Before he try if loam or sand
> Be still remaining in the place
> Delved for each polisht pillar's base.

[1] C. H. Herford, *The Age of Wordsworth*, p. 283.

> With skilful eye and fit device
> Thou raisest every edifice,
> Whether in sheltered vale it stand
> Or overlook the Dardan strand,
> Amid the cypresses that mourn
> Laodameia's love forlorn.

The advice is sufficiently trite. It appears less so, in the rather better verse of the "Epistle to the Author of 'Festus'":

> Some see but sunshine, others see but gloom,
> Others confound them strangely, furiously;
> Most have an eye for colour, few for form.
> Imperfect is the glory to *create*,
> Unless on our creation we can look
> And see that all is good; we then may rest.
> In every poem train the leading shoot;
> Break off the suckers. Thought erases thought,
> As numerous sheep erase each other's print
> When spungy moss they press or sterile sand.
> Blades thickly sown want nutriment and droop,
> Although the seed be sound, and rich the soil;
> Thus healthy-born ideas, bedded close,
> By dreaming fondness perish overlain.

This is far more provocative, challenging, as it does, that other precept of the period, to 'load every rift with ore'. And yet the principle applied in the lines to Wordsworth and in these to Bailey is identical. We find it more provocative here, because, in addressing Wordsworth, Landor uses a trite architectural metaphor for quite commonplace ideas about the need for structure in longer poems; whereas in the lines to Bailey he seems to imply that a short poem requires structure no less. And we are more willing, I think, to consider the structure of an ode or an epic than of a lyric or epigram. Just for that reason, perhaps, it is more salutary to examine Landor's theory and practice in his shorter poems. And I shall here not trouble myself with "Gebir" and the longer narratives, except to record my opinion that these poems, like the shorter ones, have been overrated by Herford and others.

To begin with, it is not hard to see why we fight shy of Landor's theories about the structure of short poems. For when Landor insists that 'ideas' must be disposed carefully about the poem, not crowded one upon another, he raises at once the question of a staple language in which those 'ideas' may be set. The staple of a poem, in this sense, is the diction of the poem. And problems of poetic diction are particularly difficult in the period of the Preface to *Lyrical Ballads*. Critics have never reached agreement about the rights and wrongs of Wordsworth's remarks on diction, and as a result no one has examined with any thoroughness the diction of our Romantic poets. This has prevented us esteeming, as we should, such different achievements as "The White Doe of Rylstone" and "The Witch of Atlas". For Landor's principles of disposition seem to me self-evidently right; and it follows that poetic diction, in the sense of a staple language for the poet, is a burning question for poets and readers in any age.

Landor's practice is another matter. The very lines in which he expounds his theory show how far he was from putting it into practice. To begin with, his word 'ideas' is peculiar, since any logical arrangement of words has meaning, and in that sense contains ideas. He cannot mean what he seems to say, that the staple, the gold ring in which the gems are set, shall be devoid of ideas, hence meaningless. And I infer that by 'ideas' Landor means rather what older critics called 'figures'. In other words, we are to find 'ideas' in this sense wherever we find in a poem any conscious rhetoric, any attempt to be striking, concentrated or elaborate beyond what we expect from conversational prose. As a matter of fact, the lines from the "Epistle to the Author of 'Festus'" are themselves highly figurative, in the way they seem to condemn. And only four of them can be said to contain no images:

> Most have an eye for colour, few for form.
> Imperfect is the glory to *create*,
> Unless on our creation we can look
> And see that all is good; we then may rest.

Here, then, if anywhere, we should find the staple language, that poetic diction which Landor seems to demand, in which figures ('ideas') shall be disposed. Yet here the language is quite indiscriminate. The first line is notably conversational, the second, with its italic, even more so. But the third and fourth, with their presumptuous echo from Genesis, are elaborate, rhetorical and literary. How can this be a staple language, or a pure diction, when in the space of four lines it veers so giddily from high to low? It betrays in particular a bewildering insecurity of *tone*. At one moment the poet is addressing us amicably in the study; at the next, he is thundering from a rostrum. How can we know how to take him? What tone can we adopt in reading the poem aloud? The golden ring is cracked; and, however fine the brilliants, we can only be distressed.

This seems to me the besetting sin of all Landor's writing, something which cancels out all his other virtues. And nearly always Landor courts disaster, as here by the italic, so elsewhere by passages of direct speech. This is the case, for instance, in the much-anthologized "Faesulan Idyll":

> I held down a branch
> And gather'd her some blossoms; since their hour
> Was come, and bees had wounded them, and flies
> Of harder wing were working their way thro'
> And scattering them in fragments under-foot.
> So crisp were some, they rattled unevolved,
> Others, ere broken off, fell into shells,
> For such appear the petals when detacht,
> Unbending, brittle, lucid, white like snow,
> And like snow not seen thro', by eye or sun:
> Yet everyone her gown received from me
> Was fairer than the first. I thought not so,
> But so she praised them to reward my care.
> I said, "You find the largest."
>   "This indeed,"
> Cried she, "is large and sweet." She held one forth,
> Whether for me to look at or to take
> She knew not, nor did I; but taking it
> Would best have solved (and this she felt) her doubt.

No doubt one censures this most sharply, by pointing to the inept handling of the blank-verse measure. But if we try to look at it still from the standpoint of diction, we have to find much to admire. The language is pro-saic in the best sense carrying precise observation—'working their way thro''; and the same language is used to a different end in the last lines, where it renders with some subtlety a moment of human contact. Even the Miltonic Latinism 'unevolved' could be saved by the strong coarseness of 'rattled'. It is true that the comparison with shells and snow is less happy, its would-be precision all on the surface. But what damns the passage is the inserted exchange of direct speech. Everything is more conversational than the conversation.[1] The movement of real speech is trimmed and elevated, as if the context were more lofty than it is. And yet the poem began loftily enough:

> Here, where precipitate Spring, with one light bound
> Into hot Summer's lusty arms, expires. . . .

The truth is that Landor merely takes no care for any consistent tone of discourse.

As a matter of fact, despite his advice to 'train the leading shoot', Landor was always prone to lose the thread of his poems, even in more obvious ways. In a poem addressed to satire, which contains more promising lines (for, like Shelley, Landor had satirical talent, but despised it), the failure with direct speech only aggravates a trailing-off into obscurity:

> Byron was not *all* Byron; one small part
> Bore the impression of a human heart.
> Guided by no clear love-star's panting light
> Thro' the sharp surges of a northern night,
> In Satire's narrow strait he swam the best,
> Scattering the foam that hist about his breast.
> He who might else have been more tender, first

---

[1] Mr. F. W. Bateson suggests that "You find the largest" is genuinely colloquial, if it is an imperative, as he thinks it is. This had not occurred to me; and I had taken it to mean "Oh, you are only looking at the big ones". At any rate we can agree that the reply is stilted.

From Scottish saltness caught his rabid thirst.
Praise Keats. . . .
                    "I think I've heard of him."
                              "With you
Shelley stands foremost."
                    . . . And his lip was blue. . . .
"I hear with pleasure any one commend
So good a soul; for Shelley is my friend."
One leaf from Southey's laurel made explode
All his combustibles. . . .
                              "An ass! by God!"

This is mere doodling. It would be hard to find anything less classical, in Landor's or any other sense.

It is unfair perhaps, to recall it. For we can adapt Herford's verdict on "Gebir" and say of its author that "though hardly a great poet, he is full of the symptoms of greatness". Nothing could be much more damaging or sadder; for, as Herford also says, "It is characteristic of Landor that he is great in detail rather than in mass".[1] In other words, the poet who tried above all things for the poem as an artifact, a whole thing cut loose from its maker, emerges as a true poet only in fragments and snatches. It is for this reason that one turns back through Landor's poems, coming across distinguished phrases by the way, and thinking, "Surely I have misjudged him". But one never has. On re-reading, the poem does not improve; it is still disastrously uneven, in the rough, unshaped. The fine writing remains irrelevant; it never adds up to an effect.

This difficulty should not arise so sharply with the epigrams. And the best of these are very good:

[1] Herford, *op. cit.* p. 273.

Clap, clap the double nightcap on!
Gifford will read you his amours,
Lazy as Scheld and cold as Don;
Kneel, and thank Heaven they are not
yours.

But this, it will be said, is to miss the point. His epigrams are important—the argument runs—because
they retrieve the epigram from flippancy and make it
once again a serious vehicle, as in the Greek Anthology.
Well, I should like to think so. But in the first place
flippancy can be serious in one sense where a solemn
triviality is not. Such graceful marginalia as the lines
"With Petrarca's Sonnets" or "On Catullus" are all
very well in their way, but not serious in the sense that
posterity need remember them. There are other epigrams that offer to be serious in the sense that they are
momentous statements, and these that are serious in
every sense often fail of their effect in the same way as
the longer poems, on the score of diction.

Leaving aside the marginalia, Landor's epigrams
can be divided for convenience into three classes. There
are in the first place the compliments ("Dirce", for instance, and most of the poems to Ianthe). Then there
are traditional commonplaces, to be expressed in novel
ways, with a seeming finality ("Rose Aylmer", "The
Leaves are falling; so am I"). And finally there are
poems which offer to be 'discoveries', original in theme
but expressed in traditional form. These last two classes
may correspond to the two functions of wit, as distinguished by Johnson in the Life of Pope.

The most famous example of the first class is the
epigram on "Dirce":

Stand close around, ye Stygian set,
    With Dirce in one boat conveyed!
Or Charon, seeing, may forget
    That he is old, and she a shade.

In the classical examples of such compliments, from the seventeenth and eighteenth centuries, we find the effect depends upon combining daring hyperbole with imperturbable urbanity:

To her, whose beauty doth excell
    Stories, wee tosse theis cupps, and fill
    Sobrietie, a sacrifice
To the bright lustre of her eyes.
Each soule that sipps this is divine:
Her beauty deifies the wine.

'Urbanity' begs at once the question of diction. For to explain how these trivia seem momentous, we have to give to 'urbanity' the meaning that Arnold gave to it, in "The Literary Influence of Academies", when he spoke of it as the tone or spirit of the centre, embodying the best of a civilization. There, of course, he spoke of such urbanity as an attribute of the best prose, and thought it no business of the poet. But such centrality seems the virtue of a pure diction in poetry, as of an Attic style in prose. And one distinguishes between Landor's compliment and Carew's by saying that in the latter speaks the voice of Caroline culture, whereas in Landor's verses nothing speaks but the voice of the poet himself. It could not be otherwise, for there was for Landor no Regency or Victorian culture to speak through his mouth, as Caroline culture spoke through Carew. Carew knew where he could find the best thought and feeling of his age—at Great Tew, or Hampton Court. It was embodied in a society, the best society of his time. By Landor's time, to speak of 'the best society' required quotation-marks. What was accounted the best was plainly not the best; and to find the best one went to Venice or Fiesole, Hampstead or Ravenna, where one found not a society but a cluster of cliques. One has to say that by Landor's day to turn an elegant compliment and make momentous poetry of it was no longer a possibility; and of course it has never been possible since.

The same is true of the second class of Landor's epigrams, his attempts at 'what oft was thought but ne'er so well expressed'. To make poetry out of moral commonplace, a poet has to make it clear that he speaks not in his own voice (that would be impertinent) but as the spokesman of a social tradition. Hence the importance of the Horatian imitation for Pope, or the imitation of Juvenal by Johnson. By employing those forms and modes, the poets spoke out of a tradition which was not merely literary; for the reading of Horace and Juvenal was a tradition of social habit in the audience they addressed, which was also the society for which they spoke. The Greek epigram was no substitute. And when Landor treats a traditional commonplace ("Past ruin'd Ilion Helen lives", "The Leaves are falling; so am I", "There is a mountain and a wood between us") his achievement seems frail and marginal, chiefly because he does not show, in the form he chooses, how traditional, how far from original, is what he wants to say. The difficulty appears very clearly in respect of what is probably the most famous of all the epigrams:

I strove with none, for none was worth my strife;
  Nature I loved, and, next to Nature, Art;
I warmed both hands before the fire of life;
  It sinks, and I am ready to depart.

Landor realized the enormity of Byron's demands for admiration, and here I think he meant to avoid it, making instead a dignified *apologia pro vita sua*, like Swift's at the end of "The Death of Dr. Swift". But instead he falls between two stools; for we do not feel, as we feel with the traditional forms of apologia, that the apologist makes a case for his own life only as one version of the universal human predicament. It is not at all clear that Landor does not regard his own life and his own nobility as something unique and special. And the reader can therefore be excused for thinking that in the four lines of Landor's epigram and the umpteen lines of "Manfred" the attitude is the same—exorbitant, immature and self-pitying.

There remains the third sort of epigram, which I have called 'Discoveries'. I have in mind the use made of this idea by De Quincey, in respect of Wordsworth:

the author who wins notice the most, is not he that perplexes men by truths drawn from fountains of absolute novelty—truths as yet unsunned, and from that cause obscure; but he that awakens into illuminated consciousness ancient lineaments of truth long slumbering in the mind, although too faint to have extorted attention. Wordsworth has brought many a truth into life both for the eye and for the understanding, which previously had slumbered indistinctly for all men.

Like Wordsworth, Landor does not discover 'truths drawn from fountains of absolute novelty'. Perhaps

Shelley does. At any rate, Landor occasionally makes discoveries of the Wordsworthian sort, not 'what oft was thought but ne'er so well expressed', but what was never consciously thought before, nor ever expressed. Even here, I think, he tries more often than he succeeds. But sometimes he can make genuine discoveries, especially about movements of the mind:

> Something (ah! tell me what) there is
> To cause that melting tone.
> I fear a thought has gone amiss
> Returning quite alone.

In this field, urbanity is of no account, as the name of Wordsworth may remind us. For it is achievement of this sort which preserves many of Wordsworth's early poems, where the diction is eccentric and the versification barely adequate. So, in the poem quoted, the diction of the first two lines is faded and decadent, but this is important only because it leads us to expect something quite different from what we are given thereafter. In other words it makes the discovery more sudden and surprising. Perhaps for this reason, the lines have been found obscure, but their bearing is plain enough. Landor catches in a touching metaphor the experience of breaking off a line of thought, surprised by a melancholy reflection. He explains the shadow falling across the face of his companion by the supposition that a thought has 'gone amiss' (i.e. broken off the train of thought of which it was a link) and 'returned alone', or, as the common metaphor has it, 'brought home' to the thinker a melancholy truth. The poem, one could say, is an exploration and a discovery of what we mean when we say "The truth was brought home to me". To give form to an experience so fugitive yet so permanently human seems to me an achievement of a high order. Unfortunately I can think of only one other case in which Landor does something comparable, in his poem "For an Urn in Thoresby Park".

There is considerable pathos in the story of Landor's life, so devoted, so disinterested, and to so little end. It is interesting and important chiefly because his attempt to put the clock back shows how inevitable was the Romantic revolution in poetic method and the conception of the poet's function. The poets had to undertake to make discoveries of truth, in some sense novel, because the poetry of truths already acknowledged depended upon conditions which no longer obtained. To make poetry out of traditional commonplace or personal compliment the poet had to write in and for a homogeneous society acknowledging strong and precise traditions of literature and manners. His awareness of such a society as his audience gave the poet the sureness of tone which comes out of a pure diction and achieves urbanity. When Landor attempted this, all the odds were against him. No such society and no such audience existed. And as a result, the great poets of the age were great in quite novel ways. Wordsworth, for instance, eschewed urbanity and made a virtue of provincialism. Shelley set out to be the discoverer in an absolute sense. Keats, when he was not the discoverer, evaded the question of a staple language by figurative luxury. And when the poets needed to be urbane (as in "Don Juan" or at the end of "The Witch of Atlas") they sought no longer an impossible purity of diction, but a sort of calculated impurity; so that urbanity since has always been ironical. Landor is the type of the poet who refuses to acknowledge the temper of his age. There is a certain magnificence in his obstinate wrong-headedness; but it did not go to produce important poems.

A POSTSCRIPT, 1966

ONE of my pleasant memories is of Kingsley Amis, when we met for the first time, telling me how he had come across *Purity of Diction in English Verse* in Swansea Public Library, and had read it with enthusiasm. What pleased me was that Amis had liked the book, not in his capacity of university teacher (as he then was), but from the point of view of himself as poet. For it was thus that I had written the book : not in the first place as a teaching-manual, nor as foundation-stone of my own career in universities (though it has usefully performed both these functions), but principally so as to understand what I had been doing, or trying to do, in the poems I had been writing. Under a thin disguise the book was, as it still is, a manifesto.

All this was at a time when Amis and I and one or two others discovered that we had been moving, each by his own route, upon a common point of view as regards the writing of poems. That point of intersection, or an area of agreement around it, came to be called The Movement, and under that title has earned itself a footnote in the literary histories, being considerably blown upon in the process. I like to think that if the group of us had ever cohered enough to subscribe to a common manifesto, it might have been *Purity of Diction in English Verse.*

It is a great pity, I think, that we did not acknowledge our common ground in some such way. Instead we were all morbidly anxious not to seem to be acting in concert. That anxiety, I'm afraid, came from a streak of aggressive philistinism that ran through all our thinking. We would not entertain for a moment any idea that poetry could be, in some degree or from some points of view, a self-justifying activity. The merest whiff of art for art's sake, and we panicked, shouting. In my book this vulgar streak shows up where I declare myself indifferent to any poem or poetic effect that cannot be shown to be "moral". Nowadays this strikes me as strident and silly. And yet I can see clearly enough how it came about, as an angry reaction from the tawdry amoralism of a London Bohemia which had destroyed Dylan Thomas, the greatest talent of the generation before ours, and had helped some journalists to cast a facile glamour over the wasted squalor of Thomas's last years. Some years later, in his learned and mordantly witty poem, "Antecedents", Charles Tomlinson wrote of the Bohemianism which grew up around the figure of Thomas as only a vulgarized reach-me-down version of the more justifiable Bohemias of the nineteenth-century in France. Tomlinson was a poet quite outside the Movement and opposed to it, though not opposed, I am glad to say, to the thesis of *Purity of Diction in English Verse*. It seems to me now that the poems of Tomlinson, the poems of Amis and others, my own poems and this essay in poetics, have at least this continuing relevance and importance—that they represent an originally passionate rejection, by one generation of British poets, of all the values of Bohemia. In some later studies I have made of the English poets of the later eighteenth century I have treated of William Cowper and John Langhorne and others in just this way, as writers who consciously spurned the depraved and depraving London Bohemia of their day, a Bohemia which destroyed the talent of Charles Churchill just as the Bohemia of the 1940s destroyed Dylan Thomas. In *Purity of Diction in English Verse* this aspect of the matter is present, if at all, only by implication. But if I tried to rescue from neglect certain eighteenth-century poets, it was because all of them, in their styles of life as in their styles of writing, turned their faces against that "way of excess" which was prescribed by their Bohemia as by ours. That there is no necessary connection between the poetic vocation on the one hand, and on the other exhibitionism, egotism, and licence—this was what my book was contending for, even when it seemed most "technical". The Bohemians hit back by calling it "puritan" or, more cleverly, "genteel."

At certain past times and in certain places I dare say Bohemia has truly been the haven that it always claims to be, for lovers and artists. We asserted that in London, in the 1940s and 1950s, it was no haven but a quicksand ; and if shunning the metropolis made us provincials, we were ready to take that risk, as William Cowper and William Wordsworth had taken it. In any case London's Bohemia counts for more in the literary life of England than Greenwich Village can count for in the literary life of the United States. This meant that ours was very much a British, even an English quarrel, and that there was no counterpart on the other side of the Atlantic to the animus which inflamed our writing. Good American readers noticed this when our poems appeared in anthologies over there, alongside American poems technically similar. Those American poems, usually more accomplished than ours, were academic in a way our poems were not, though "academic" was another of the disparagements thrown at us. For the Americans the academy was a refuge from the Philistines; for us, an alternative to Bohemia.

In some of the poets of the Movement, provincialism and philistinism added up to impenitent insularity; they were Little-Englanders, and were castigated for it, rightly. And not many of them would have given such weight as I did, and still do, to the opinions of a figure of the international *avant-garde*, Ezra Pound. All the same, I seem to detect that not only the struggle against Bohemia, but more generally an approach to poetry by way of its diction, comes more naturally to British writers and readers than to American. This is true at least if "diction" is taken in the sense I argue for—the sense in which, though all poems use language, only some employ a diction. (And I may as well say that I still think this the only strict and useful meaning for the word.) I argued that among the pressures which a poet must respond to, if he is employing a diction, are pressures of class-usage—and of *speech*-usage, to the extent that all poems are written to be spoken, unless written to be sung. Every one knows that British society is class-ridden, and that in Britain the badge of class is speech;

and that in American society this is not so, or not to the same degree. And so one might find reasons why there may be nuances of poetic diction to which the Englishman is sensitive because of his social conditioning, in a way no American is. There is nothing chauvinistic about such speculations. T. S. Eliot in one of his last essays decided that we were confronted with an unprecedented phenomenon: two distinct literatures, British and American, inside one language. If this is so (and leaving aside the troublesome actualities or probabilities of Anglo-Welsh, Anglo-Scottish, New Zealand literature, Trinidadian and so on), it cannot be insular chauvinism to applaud the emergence of emphases which do in fact distinguish one of the literatures in English from the other. It would be delightful if a living affinity with masters of prosaic diction such as Cowper and Crabbe, bearing in mind of course the Englishness of their subject-matter, were for a time to distinguish the British idiom in verse from the American, and British taste from American taste. Unfortunately, however, those of us who some years ago were castigating British taste for its insularity have lately got more than we bargained for, and we see with dismay young British writers slavishly imitating American styles of writing which have meaning and validity only in relation to specifically Amer can predicaments.

Fourteen years is not too short a time for retrospect and afterthought. Indeed the England of the 1950s is in some ways extraordinarily remote already. It was at some time quite late in that decade that John Wain objected to the pervasive "lack of style" in English

o

life; and I remember privately but readily endorsing his irritation. Yet in 1966 "style"—in clothes, in behaviour, in haircuts, in the theatre, in pop-music— is one thing that the self-regarding Britain of Carnaby Street is not short of. If I were now writing *Purity of Diction in English Verse* I should need to take greater pains than I did in 1952, to distinguish the literary styles I was analyzing from what passes for style in the hectic circles that invent or exploit or tamely follow the dictates of the "with it". I could not now take it for granted so much as I did then, that the only elegance worth bothering with, in life or in art, is that which is heartfelt.

Donald Davie,
October 1966

PATHOS AND CHASTITY IN THOMAS GRAY AND THOMAS PARNELL

I HAVE tried to show that Goldsmith and Wordsworth are at one in asserting that highly figurative writing is more inimical to the pathetic strain than to the sublime. Like most of the contentions of criticism, this cannot be proved. But it may be worth while to present an example which seems to bear out this contention.

Goldsmith admired the work of Thomas Parnell, a neglected minor poet of Pope's circle;[1] and he thought Parnell's "Night-piece on Death" superior to Gray's "Elegy in a Country Churchyard". Johnson disagreed politely, and no doubt we must side with him, for Gray's poem is a more ambitious piece. But certainly Parnell avoids some of the traps into which Gray falls.

William Empson criticizes a stanza from the "Elegy":

> Full many a gem of purest ray serene
> The dark, unfathomed caves of ocean bear;
> Full many a flower is born to blush unseen
> And waste its sweetness on the desert air.

[1] There is a fatuous crib from Parnell in Goldsmith's *Threnodia Augustalis*. Death speaks in Parnell's Night-piece:

> "When Men my Scythe and Darts supply,
> How great a King of Fears am I!"

And Goldsmith starts a song:

> "When vice my dart and scythe supply
> How great a king of terrors I! . . ."

Mr. Empson points out that "a gem does not mind being in a cave and a flower prefers not to be picked; we feel that the man is like the flower, as short-lived, natural and valuable, and this tricks us into feeling that he is better off without opportunities".

Parnell's version of the 'village Hampdens' is as follows:

> The flat smooth Stones that bear a Name,
> The Chissel's slender Help to Fame,
> (Which ere our Sett of Friends decay
> Their frequent Steps may wear away.)
> A middle Race of Mortals own,
> Men, half ambitious, all unknown.

While it may be true, as Johnson says, that Parnell's verse falls short of Gray's in 'dignity, variety and originality of sentiment', it has here the advantage of keeping the subject soberly in view. If the line read '*un*ambitious' the way would be clear: "Unworried by worldly competition, these men were happy". Or if it read '*all* ambitious', it would spark another ready response: "Men in this humble sphere are worldly as we are, and we, like them, shall be unknown". Gray, while purporting to say the second, really says the first. Parnell's prosaic 'half-ambitious' says neither, and his pathos is free of any trickery. The treacherous ambiguity comes in with the metaphors.

'STRENGTH' AND 'EASE' IN SEVENTEENTH-CENTURY CRITICISM

SOME of our difficulty in dealing with the abundant good verse of the first part of the seventeenth century derives from the poverty of literary criticism in this period. Outside Jonson's "Discoveries" and Hobbes' essay on "Gondibert" we look in vain for anything to tell us how the men of the period regarded the poetry they and their contemporaries were writing. And as there is no way of taking this poetry on its own valuation, we have to provide scales of our own—'Cavalier lyrists', 'metaphysicals', 'the marinist tradition', 'the line of wit'. None of these labels would have made sense to any of the poets to whom we attach them.

If there is no criticism in the period, there are clues to be found in the poetry itself to two terms which would have made sense to them. From title-pages, poems of dedication, and votive offerings to poetic masters, we can extricate the terms 'strength' and 'ease'; and we can deduce that it was in these terms that the poets discussed their own and each other's verse. Our difficulty lies in trying to define, on this meagre and fragmentary evidence, what was meant by each of these words. And in the case of 'ease' this question is probably insoluble, since the meaning appears to fluctuate between a smooth fluency in numbers and a quite different, though related, quality of social demeanour, the 'sprezzatura' of Castiglione and the Sidneyan ideal, a potent influence at least as late as Lovelace. 'Strength' can be defined more closely, and it is in 'strength' that I am chiefly interested; but since the terms are frequently opposed, and the one seems to strike off from the other, it seems advisable to try to trace them both together.

In "Discoveries", Jonson censures both extremes, both too much strength and too much ease. You shall have, he says—

Others, that in composition are nothing, but what is rough, and broken: Quae per salebras, altaque saxa cadunt. And if it would come gently, they trouble it of purpose. They would not have it run without rubs, as if that stile were more strong and manly, that stroke the eare with a kind of uneven(n)esse. These men erre not by chance, but knowingly, and willingly; they are like men that affect a fashion by themselves, have some singularity in a Ruffe, Cloake, or Hat-band; or their beards, specially cut to provoke beholders, and set a marke upon themselves. They would be reprehended, while they are look'd on. And this vice, one that is in authority with the rest, loving, delivers over to them to bee imitated: so that oft-times the faults which he fell into, the others seeke for: This is the danger, when vice becomes a Precedent.

Others there are, that have no composition at all; but a kind of tuneing, and riming fall, in what they write. It runs and slides, and onely makes a sound. Womens-Poets they are call'd: as you have womens-Taylors.

"They write a verse, as smooth, as soft, as creame;
    In which there is no torrent, nor scarce streame."

You may sound these wits, and find the depth of them, with your middle finger. They are Creame-bowle, or but puddle deepe.[1]

This position, from which not 'strong', 'manly', 'rough' on the one side, nor 'smooth', 'easy', on the other, are

[1] Jonson, "Discoveries": *Works*, ed. Herford and Simpson, vol. viii, p. 585.

praiseworthy in themselves, was probably given lip-service throughout the period.

Towards the end of the century, Jonson is echoed by Dryden in "An Essay of Dramatic Poesy". Crites declares that he has 'a mortal apprehension of two poets':

" 'Tis easy to guess whom you intend," said Lisideuis; "and without naming them, I ask you, if one of them does not perpetually pay us with clenches upon words, and a certain clownish kind of raillery? if now and then he does not offer at a catachresis or Clevelandism, wresting and torturing a word into another meaning: in fine, if he be not one of those whom the French would call un mauvais buffon; one that is so much a well-willer to the satire, that he spares no man; and though he cannot strike a blow to hurt any, yet ought to be punished for the malice of the action, as our witches are justly hanged, because they think themselves so; and suffer deservedly for believing they did mischief, because they meant it." "You have described him," said Crites, "so exactly, that I am afraid to come after you with my other extremity of poetry. He is one of those who, having had some advantage of education and converse, knows better than the other what a poet should be, but puts it into practice mure unluckily than any man; his style and matter are everywhere alike: he is the most calm, peaceable writer you ever read: he never disquiets your passions with the least concernment, but still leaves you in as even a temper as he found you; he is a very Leveller in poetry; he creeps along with ten little words in every line, and helps out his numbers with *For to*, and *Unto*, and all the pretty expletives he can find, till he drags them to the end of another line; while the sense is left tired half way behind it: he doubly starves all his verses, first for want of thought and then of expression; his poetry neither has wit in it, nor seems to have it; like him in Martial:

'Pauper videri Cinna vult, et est pauper.' " [1]

[1] *Essays of John Dryden*, selected and edited by W. P. Ker, vol. i, pp. 31, 32. The two poets discussed are identified as, on the one hand, Robert Wild, on the other (perhaps) Flecknoe.

Dryden's prose is more loose-limbed, and his fancy more fantastic, but it is plain that his two 'extremities of poetry' are roughly the same as Jonson's.

Between Jonson's essay and Dryden's, this notion of a balance to be struck between too much strength and too much ease was the principle on which all critical perspective was aligned. The terms 'soft' or 'smooth' and 'strong' were habitually opposed:

> His Muse is soft, as sweet, and though not strong,
> Pathetic, lively, all on fire, and young.[1]

But the poets can be seen to group themselves, according as they more esteem the strong and masculine style, or the smooth and easy. And these groupings are not always those wished upon the poets by later historians.

A spokesman of those poets who most admired ease may have been Suckling. In "Sessions of the Poets", he censures Godolphin for his 'strength':

> During these troubles in the Court was hid
> One that Apollo soon mist, little Cid;
> And having spied him, call'd him out of the throng,
> And advis'd him in his ear not to write so strong.

This attitude is shared by Earle, discussing Lord Falkland:

> Dr. Earles would not allow him to be a good poet, though a great witt; he writ not a smoth verse, but a greate deal of sense.[2]

It is not surprising, on the other hand, that Godolphin appears as the spokesman of the 'strong', using the term as one of unqualified praise:

[1] "L. B.", prefatory poem to "Arcadius and Sepha", by William Bosworth, 1651: Saintsbury, *Caroline Poets*, vol. ii, p. 528.

[2] Aubrey, *Brief Lives*, Life of Falkland.

APPENDIX B

This Work had been proportion'd to our Sight,
Had you but knowne with some allay to Write,
And not preserv'd your Authors Strength and Light.

But you so crush those Odors, so dispense
Those rich perfumes, you make them too intense
And such (alas) as too much please our Sense.

We fitter are for sorrows, then such Love;
Iosiah falls, and by his fall doth move
Teares from the people, Mourning from above.

Iudah, in her Iosiah's Death, doth dye,
All Springs of grief are opened to supply
Streames to the torrent of this Elegy. . . .[1]

And again later in the same poem:

> Others translate, but you the Beames collect
> Of your inspired Authors, and reflect
> Those heavenly Rais with new and strong effect.

The disagreement between these two bodies of opinion did not remain so gentlemanly and mild. Spirits became partisan, and as usual when controversy becomes a little heated both opinions became distorted and extreme. From the first, other terms began to cluster around 'strength' on the one hand, 'ease' on the other. 'Ease' degenerated into 'smoothness':

Sucklyn and Carew, I must confess, wrote some few things smoothly enough, but as all they did in this kind was not very considerable, so 'twas a little later than the earliest pieces of Mr. Waller.[2]

And 'strength', which had from the first been con-

---

[1] "To my very much honoured Friend Mr. George Sandys upon his Paraphrase on the Poeticall Parts of the Bible", *The Poems of Sidney Godolphin* (ed. William Dighton, 1931), p. 66.
[2] Preface to *Posthumous Poems of Edmund Waller*, 1690.

nected with 'the masculine style',[1] now became the same as 'Clevelandism':

And now instead of that strenuous masculine style which breatheth in this author, we have only an enervous effeminate froth offered, as if they had taken the salivating pill before they set pen to paper. You must hold your breath in the perusal lest the jest vanish by blowing on.[2]

When, as we saw from Dryden, 'Clevelandism' became a term of reproach, 'strength' too was a term thoroughly in disrepute:

To this palpable darkness I may also add the ambitious obscurity of expressing more than is perfectly conceived or perfect conception in fewer words than it requires, which expressions, though they have had the honour to be called strong lines, are indeed no better than riddles, and, not only to the reader but also after a little time to the writer himself, dark and troublesome.[3]

And soon 'strength' became a simple gibe:

He'll take a scant piece of coarse Sense, and stretch it on the Tenterhooks of half a score Rhimes, until it crack that you may see through it, and it rattle like a Drum-Head. When you see his Verses hanged up in Tobacco-Shops, you may say, in defiance of the Proverb, that the weakest does not always go to the Wall; for 'tis well known the Lines are strong enough, and in that Sense may justly take the Wall of any, that have been written in our Language.[4]

It becomes obvious that the confusions engendered by this word 'strength' are becoming unmanageable.

[1] Cf. Carew on Donne. An Elegie upon the Death of Dr. Donne.

[2] Preface to "Clievelandi Vindiciae", 1677 (Saintsbury, *Caroline Poets*, vol. iii, p. 18).

[3] Thomas Hobbes, essay on "Gondibert" (1651).

[4] Samuel Butler, *Characters*, ed. A. R. Waller (Cambridge, 1908), p. 52: "A Small Poet".

Hobbes, Jonson, Godolphin and the anonymous apologist for Cleveland seem not to be speaking of the same thing. And what are we to make of such collocations as 'the strength of his fancy'?—

> The strength of his fancy, and the shadowing of it in words, he taketh from Mr. Marlow in his Hero and Leander. . . .[1]

Confusion is worse confounded when, in the next century, Pope and Dr. Johnson are found applauding Denham as 'strong':

> The 'strength of Denham' which Pope so emphatically mentions, is to be found in many lines and couplets, which convey much meaning in few words, and exhibit the sentiment with more weight than bulk.[2]

And for chaos to come again, we may cite John Drinkwater:

> 'Apollo', says Suckling in a doggerel passage of the 'Sessions of the Poets', calling 'little Cid' 'out of the throng', advised him 'not to write so strong'. Unless the warning had some special allusion that now escapes us, Apollo could not well have talked greater nonsense. Violence is the quality furthest removed from Godolphin's reserved and modest muse. A little access of vigour was what he most needed. Not vigour of conscience or invention, but of speech. He remained his own debtor for an occasional transport of vehemence that might have loosened up the whole current of his poetry.[3]

---

[1] "R. C." To the Reader: prefixed to "Arcadius and Sepha" (1651).

[2] Dr. Johnson, "Denham": *Lives of the Poets*.

[3] John Drinkwater, *The Poems of Sidney Godolphin* (ed. Dighton), Introduction, p. xi. It may be remarked that the other side of the controversy is also fruitful of confusions, though not to such an extent. Thus, in respect of the 'ease-smoothness-sweetness' group of terms, it may be pointed out that in seventeenth-century parlance it is possible for verse to be easy, smooth and laboured all at once. 'Laboured' is not a term of dispraise; cf. Saintsbury, *Caroline Poets*, vol. ii, p. 529: "On these laboured poems of the deceased Author, Mr. William Bosworth".

Although we may not hope to be able to pin down every usage, we may come near to the 'special allusion', which escaped Mr. Drinkwater.

For at least it is apparent that whatever 'strength' may be, it is not what Drinkwater supposes, "a transport of vehemence that might have loosened up the whole current". 'Strength' is not a 'loosening' but a 'tightening'; it is a matter of compression and concentration. And Johnson therefore used the word with propriety when he applied it to Denham, and disengaged it from the hyperbolical conceit with which it had been identified. Donne achieves concentration by way of hyperbole; Denham by means of syntax. And both are 'strong'.

INDEX

INDEX